LIPIKA

RABINDRANATH TAGORE

Lipika

PROSE POEMS

Translated
and with an Introduction by

AUROBINDO BOSE

Rupa . Co

First published in 1977 by
Peter Owen Limited
20 Holland Park Avenue London W11 3QU

First British Commonwealth edition 1977

First in Rupa Paperback 2002

Published by
Rupa . Co
7/16, Ansari Road, Daryaganj,
New Delhi 110 002

Offices at:
15 Bankim Chatterjee Street, Kolkata 700 073
135 South Malaka, Allahabad 211 001
PG Solanki Path, Lamington Road, Mumbai 400 007
36, Kutty Street, Nungambakkam, Chennai 600 034
Surya Shree, B-6, New 66, Shankara Park,
Basavangudi, Bangalore 560 004
3-5-612, Himayat Nagar, Hyderabad 500 029

Translated from the Bengali

Printed in India by
Rekha Printers Pvt. Ltd., A-102/1 Okhla Industrial Area, New Delhi-110020

To the sacred memory of Sir J. C. Bose FRS and Lady Bose, in whose love I grew up as a child, and who demanded from their friend *Rabi* a new story every day during their visit to his houseboat on the river Padma.

CONTENTS

Contents

The Introduction is drawn from 'A Life of Rabindranath Tagore' by Aurobindo Bose, which appeared in *The Herald of Spring* (1957), and appears by kind permission of the publishers, John Murray Ltd.

INTRODUCTION

Rabindranath Tagore: The Man and the Poet

Rabindranath Tagore was born in Calcutta on 6 May, 1861, and died on 7 August, 1941. His grandfather, Prince Dwarkanath Tagore, was a friend of the great Indian religious reformer Raja Ramohan Roy, and one of the first Indians to travel to Europe, where he was received with great honour at the Courts of both France and England. His father, Devendranath Tagore, unlike the grandfather, was not a man of the world but a mystic and a religious leader. The Tagore family have contributed greatly to the cultural life of Bengal, and the debt that Bengal owes them is immeasurable.

From this family have come poets, artists and musicians, the greatest of them being Rabindranath, the youngest of a number of gifted brothers and sisters.

Beyond irregular attendance at two or three schools for very short periods – of which he had most unpleasant memories – he studied at home with private tutors. But he read much by himself when still a child, particularly the classics of medieval Bengali and Sanskrit literature, and it did not worry him greatly if he did not understand everything. The sounds of the words and the lilt of the metre, combined with what he could guess of the meaning of Sanskrit words from his fairly thorough knowledge of Bengali, conjured up for him pictures of wonderful beauty.

In later life, partly with the help of a German missionary lady but mainly by his own efforts, he managed to learn enough German to be able to read Heine's *Buch der Lieder* and Goethe's *Faust*. At the age of seventeen, he was sent to England, where he studied English literature at University College, London, under Professor Henry Morley. However, unlike many western-educated Indians of his generation, he did not write a line of English until he was fifty – and then almost by accident. After a severe illness, doctors had advised him to take a sea-trip, so he sailed for England in 1912 and, during the voyage, made some translations from his poems for his English friends. When he arrived in England, this tiny sheaf came into the hands of the Irish poet W. B. Yeats, who was deeply moved by its beauty and depth of mystical feeling. In the autumn of 1912 these poems were published under the title of *Gitanjali* (Song Offerings) with an introduction by Yeats, bringing Tagore the Nobel Prize in the following year.

When Tagore was born, Bengal was astir with new life, which found expression in three great movements – religious, literary and national – all of which were later to be enriched by the poet's own unique contributions. The religious movement was started by the 'great-hearted man of gigantic intelligence', as Tagore calls him, Raja Ramohan Roy (1774-1833), founder of the *Brahma Samaj* or 'Theistic Church of India'. Roy tried to reopen the channel of spiritual life which had become obstructed and fixed in external practices lacking spiritual significance. His was a strictly monotheistic religion, based upon the teachings of the *Upanishads*.[1] He also believed in the harmony of religions and taught reverence for all the great religions of the world. In politics he was a true democrat, working hard for the political and social advancement of his country. He exerted the greatest influence in moulding Tagore's own ideals, and Tagore later expressed his profound indebtedness to this great man in innumerable addresses. Tagore's father, *Maharshi*[2] Devendranath, became the leader of the *Bramah Samaj* after Ramohan Roy's death, and as a result the Tagore family was completely ostracized by orthodox Hindus. This, according to the poet, was a blessing for him, for it saved him from blindly imitating the past.

The second movement, a literary one, was heralded by the great novelist Bankim Chandra Chatterjee (1838-84), who breathed new life into the moribund literature of Bengal, 'fettered by a rhetoric rigid as death.' Tagore says of him:

> He lifted the dead weight of ponderous forms from our language and with a touch of his magic aroused our literature from her age-long sleep. What a vision of beauty she revealed to us when she awoke in the fullness of her strength and grace.

The third was the National Movement, which embraced more than purely political ideals. It expressed a spirit of revolt and self-assertion against the political as well as the cultural dominance of the West. A generation of Indians had grown up under a system of alien education and had blindly rejected their Indian cultural inheritance in religion, art and social customs, copying the West instead. The National Movement set out to rediscover the soul of India, reviving the arts and crafts, starting new industries, bringing new life into decaying villages. It was not a reactionary but a revolutionary movement.

All three movements found their votaries and active supporters in the Tagore family, among the poet's much older brothers and cousins. In this challenging and invigorating atmosphere the boy Rabindranath grew up, absorbing the music, drama and poetry that often filled the air of the great Tagore mansion; and here, while still in his teens, began his poetic apprenticeship. This atmosphere gave him above all the freedom to experiment, untrammelled by any hide-bound literary conventions. He also read extensively, both in the literature of his own country and that of Europe. From this time on until almost the end of his life, a steady stream of poetry, drama, short stories, novels, literary criticism, social and political essays, religious and philosophical discourses poured steadily from his pen.

Until his fortieth year, Tagore was almost entirely engrossed in literary work. He then turned his mind to the problems of children's education, which had always concerned him deeply, especially as he was totally out of sympathy with the existing system, deploring its emphasis on the mere acquisition of knowledge at the expense of other vital needs of the growing child. He wrote:

> We have come to this world to accept it, not merely to know it. We may become powerful by knowledge, but we attain fullness by sympathy. The highest education is that which does not merely give us information but makes our life grow, in harmony with all existence. But we find that this education of sympathy is not only systematically ignored in schools, but is severely repressed. It is a

> mere method of discipline which refuses to take the individual into account. It is designed for grinding out uniform results. Is not the crisis of modern civilization mainly due to the over-emphasis we have put on the intellectual development of men and the disregard of what one may call the 'education of the heart'?

In contrast to this, the school Tagore wanted to establish in the heart of the country was to be a place where

> men have gathered for the highest purpose in life, in the peace of nature, where life is not merely meditative, but fully awake in its activities, where boys' minds are not being perpetually drilled into believing that the self-idolatry of the nation is the truest ideal for them to accept; where they are bidden to realize man's world as God's Kingdom to whose citizenship they have to aspire; where the sunrise and sunset and the silent glory of stars are not daily ignored; where nature's festivities of flowers and fruits have their joyous recognition from man; and where the young and the old, the teacher and the student, sit at the same table to partake of their daily food, and the food of their daily life.

The school Tagore founded in the heart of the country in 1901, was one of the pioneer co-educational establishments in India. Here the pupils, who included his own sons, not only pursued their intellectual studies but also learnt carpentry, weaving and pottery, acted the poet's plays and sang the songs he composed specially for the seasonal festivals. Moreover, what began as an experimental school inspired by the ancient Indian ideal of the *ashram*[3], grew and developed with the growth of Tagore's own mind, ultimately becoming the international university known today as *Vishva-Bharati*[4]. For its motto, Tagore adopted the Sanskrit text: There where the whole world unites in a nest (*Yatra Visvam bhavaty eka-nidam*).

Around the age of forty, he also became deeply involved in the National Movement and was successively President of the Bengal Provincial Conference (a branch of the Indian National Congress) and Chairman of the Reception Committee of the Calcutta session of the Indian National Congress. His political addresses, which he delivered on many occasions, aroused nation-wide interest, and he poured out the pent-up patriotism of his countrymen in electrifying song after song. But as the National Movement became more intense and took on a more bitter form (it was at this period that the Terrorist Movement first raised its head in Bengal), Tagore became disillusioned and suddenly retired from the political field. He was bitterly criticized for this action by his countrymen, but remained silent.

I have tried to give an idea of Tagore the man, whose many-sided personality – poet, religious mystic, educationalist and lover of children, patriot and man of action – suggests to me a great similarity with Goethe. Both were supreme poets who immeasurably enriched their national literature, and both reflected in their lives the ideal of a fully integrated human being. Goethe, the poet, held high office at a German court and was a great pedagogue (as his novel *Wilhelm Meister* shows) as well as a serious scientist, interested in geology, zoology and physics. Tagore, too, included science among his many interests.[5] He was a life-long friend of the eminent Indian scientist Sir Jagadis Ch. Bose, and almost always the first to whom the latter communicated his exciting botanical discoveries (how well I remember, when still a college student, their long conferences in Bose's study and his rueful comment: 'Rabi, a great scientist has been lost in you). But more than this versatility, it is their great humanity, transcending the narrow limits of nationalism, which appeals to me in both Goethe and Tagore. Sometimes, half joking, I would say to Tagore: 'I think the spirit of Goethe has been reincarnated in you.' At which he would smile impishly and reply: 'Who knows?'

I now come to Tagore's poetry about which I feel the least competent to write, having spent my life as a spectroscopist and an atomic physicist. But my great love of Tagore's work prompts me to set down these few thoughts for the reader, in the hope that he will then go directly to the source and quench his thirst there.

Tagore began writing poetry in early adolescence and continued until the very last day of his life. There is no genre in literature which he did not attempt successfully, although posterity will remember him chiefly as a poet and composer of songs. (These last, alas, can only be known and appreciated by the men and women of his *Sonarbangla*, or golden Bengal, as he sings in one of his songs.) He had a deep love of nature, and his lyrics on this subject often have the intensity of love songs. His first book of lyrics, *Evening Songs*, reflects all the sadness, pain and vagueness of an adolescent soul struggling for expression. He does not deny the charge made against him by critics that his songs were vague, misty and shadowy, but rejects the suggestion that they were deliberately affected:[6]

> The fortunate possessor of good eyesight is apt to sneer at the youth with glasses, as if he wears them for ornament. . . . The nebula is not outside the universe – it merely represents a stage in creation; and to leave out all poetry which has not attained definiteness would not bring us to the truth of literature. If any phase of man's nature has found true expression, it is worth preserving – it may be cast aside only if not expressed truly. . . . There is a duality in man. . . . When the outward life fails to harmonize with the inner, the dweller within is hurt, and his pain manifests itself in the outer consciousness in a manner which it is difficult to name or even to describe – its cry is more akin to an inarticulate wail than to words with more precise meaning. . . . These *Evening Songs* are the history of that struggle. As in all creation, so in poetry, there is the opposition of forces. If the divergence is too wide, or the unison too close, there is, it seems to me, no room for poetry. Where the pain of discord strives to attain and express its resolution into harmony, there does poetry break forth into music, as breath through a flute.

Evening Songs was succeeded soon after by *Morning Songs*, poems composed when Tagore was not yet twenty, as a result of his first mystical experience. To quote his own words:

> One morning I happened to be standing on the verandah looking that way [the end of the street, with trees visible]. . . . The sun was just rising through the leafy tops of those trees. As I continued to gaze, all of a sudden a covering seemed to fall away from my eyes, and I found the world bathed in a wonderful radiance, with waves of beauty and joy swelling on every side. This radiance pierced in a

moment through the folds of sadness and despondency which had accumulated over my heart, and flooded it with this universal light. That very day the poem 'The Awakening of the Waterfall' gushed forth and coursed on like a veritable cascade. The poem came to an end, but the curtain did not fall upon the joyous aspect of the universe. And it came to me so that no person or thing in the world seemed to me trivial or unpleasing.[7]

Another important landmark in tracing the inner development of the young poet's mind is 'The Echo'. Of this poem Tagore writes:

> When from the original fount in the depths of the universe streams of melody are sent forth abroad, their echo is reflected in our heart from the faces of our beloved and the other beauteous things around us. It must be, as I suggested, this echo which we love, and not the things themselves from which it happens to be reflected; for that which one day we scarce deign to glance at may be, on another, the very thing which claims our whole devotion. I had so long viewed the world with external vision only, and so had been unable to see its universal aspect of joy. When of a sudden, from some innermost depth of my being, a ray of light found its way out, it spread over and illuminated for me the whole universe, which then no longer appeared like heaps of things and happenings, but was disclosed to my sight as one whole. This experience seemed to tell me of the stream of melody issuing from the very heart of the universe and spreading over space and time, re-echoing thence as waves of joy which flow right back to the source.[8]

This pure source, which welled in song, became a river broadening its banks and flowing through many lands until it reached the ocean with music both solemn and grave. It has been said that the mark of the truly great man is his capacity to remain a child – ever growing, ever changing. So we find Tagore never satisfied by what he has already achieved, always experimenting and seeking new forms of expression. He left behind the old sonorous forms of Sanskritic Bengali[9] for the simple, unadorned style of spoken Bengali, and in his last years invented a medium between poetry and prose, which he called prose poems. Late in life, also, having been privileged himself by being born into a rich and aristocratic family, he inclined towards socialism and, in a poem written only seven months before he died, confesses:

Therefore I accept the charge
That is brought against me –
The incompleteness of my songs.
I know my songs,
Though they have walked on many paths,
Have not moved everywhere.
That poet who is the peasant's friend,
Who has earned his trust through word and deed,
And who is nearer the earth –
His singing it is I wait to hear.

Thus Tagore, the mystic and the prophet, the wise man of the East in flowing robes (the picture held dear by so many elderly dowagers of the twenties!), becomes the poet to whom the love of man for man becomes the highest form of worship. He writes short stories in which the hero is an aetheist who lives by the light of his reason and follows the dictates of his conscience. Agnostic friends of mine have been cheered by poems of this kind, which I translated for them, thinking that they had at last succeeded in bringing the 'mystic' Tagore into their fold – but they were mistaken. These later works only showed the increasing charity and tolerance in a mind already tolerant, and the poet's deeper understanding of the religion of humanism. Yet in his heart he remained a true son of the *rishis* (sages) of ancient India, who sang:

Out of that great joy[10] the world is born,
Through that great joy the world is kept going,
And into that great joy they enter after death.

NOTES

[1] Sanskrit religious treatises dating from c. 1000 BC.

[2] The title by which his countrymen addressed him, meaning 'The Sage'.

[3] Forest sanctuary.

[4] *Vishva* in Sanskrit means the universe, *Bharati* means wisdom.

[5] He was the author of *Vishva-Parichay* (Introduction to the Universe), the best popular scientific book in Bengali.

[6] *My Reminiscences* by Rabindranath Tagore, (Macmillan), p. 212.

[7] Ibid., p. 217.

[8] Ibid., p. 223.

[9] The written language in my schooldays.

[10] Ananda.

TRANSLATOR'S NOTE

With *Lipika*, published in 1921, Tagore introduced a new genre into Bengali, which was to set the fashion for many young writers – that of the unrhymed prose poem broken up into long and short passages, like the English version of his *Gitanjali*. Many of these gem-like sketches come from the world of myths and fairy-tales (*rupkatha*). A number treat of the relationship between man and woman – its playful and its serious aspect – and show the elusive yet timeless quality of love. Others consider the futility of running after material possessions and measuring worth in concrete and materialist terms. All are characterised by a combination of subtle humour and lightness of touch with depth of feeling.

In addition to the twenty-seven poems from *Lipika*, I have included a number of other pieces in the same genre. To round off the collection and to show once again the many-sided nature of Tagore's genius, I have added two appendixes containing a letter from the poet on the subject of education and a selection of poems from *On My Birthday*.

I should like to thank the *Vishva-Bharati* for permission to translate these stories from *Lipika*. My sincere thanks are also due to my friend, the late F. L. Lukas, Reader in English at the University of Cambridge, for his careful reading of my manuscript and to my editor at Peter Owen, Mrs Beatrice Musgrave, for her part in making this book.

Ecole d'Humanité,
Goldern, Switzerland
1977

Aurobindo Bose

The poems numbered 1–28 in this selection appeared in the original Bengali edition of *Lipika* and numbers in brackets refer to page numbers in that edition. The sources and page numbers (where applicable) of the remaining poems are also given in brackets.

Lipika

[1]

1 *The Trodden Path*

This is the trodden Path.

It has come from the heart of the forest to the fields, from the fields to the river's edge by the pier beneath the shade of the banyan tree, then from the ruined pier on the other bank to the village, until, skirting the linseed fields along the mango glade and the lotus pond, it gets lost in some village.

So many have trod this path – some passed me by, some kept me company; some I saw from a distance, some had their faces veiled, some did not; some went to fetch water, some returned with their pitchers filled.

Now the day has ended and darkness falls.

Once I felt that this path was mine – wholly mine!

Now I find that I had permission to tread it just once and no more.

Passing the lemon grove, the village pond, the temple pier, the alluvial land, the cowshed, the granary, I meet familiar faces, hear familiar voices and exclaim:

'So, here you are!'

All this will not happen again!

This is the path to move forward on – not the one on which to return.

In today's grey twilight I turned back once, and the path appeared to me as a wreath of stanzas of forgotten footsteps sung to a classic tune.

All the travellers who have trod this path through the Ages – their history is drawn in but one short line in its dust.

That one single line has travelled from the land of sunrise to the land of sunset, from one great gate to another.

'O trodden Path! Do not keep voiceless the histories of countless lives bound within your dust. I have my ears to the ground – whisper your message to me.'

The path, pointing its finger to the dark curtain of the night, remains silent.

'O trodden Path! The thoughts, the desires of countless men – where have they gone?'

The dumb path does not speak, but only points its finger from the land of sunrise to the land of sunset.

'O trodden Path! The footsteps that once poured upon you like the rain of flowers, are they nowhere to be found today?'

Does the path know its own end – where the withered flowers and silenced song arrive?

And where, in the light of stars, is the festival of unquenched Sorrows?

The dumb path does not speak, but only points its finger from the land of sunrise to the land of sunset.

'O trodden Path! The footsteps that once poured upon you like the rain of flowers, are they nowhere to be found today?'

Does the path know its own end – where the withered flowers and silenced song arrive?

And where, in the light of stars, is the festival of unquenched Sorrows?

2 *A Cloudy Day*

In India, a rainy day during the monsoon is like a spring day in Europe. Gone is the scorching, all-devouring heat of summer, and the trees are bare as in Europe in winter. Then, suddenly, the monsoon arrives with her cool breezes. Man breathes again, and his thoughts turn to love, to the desire to do nothing but dream. This is the background the Western reader must conjure up to appreciate what follows. *(Translator)*

Each day is filled with work and all around me there are crowds of people.

Daily I feel that in the day's work, in the day's intercourse with people, all that there is to say has been said – nothing more remains.

One has no time to become aware of what remains unsaid deep down in one's heart.

This morning the sky is heavy with mass upon mass of clouds.

Even today work lies ahead, and men are all about me.

But I feel that what is within me cannot be completely uttered to the world outside.

Man has crossed the oceans, climbed the mountains; digging down into the depths of the netherworld, he has stolen gems and precious stones and brought them to the surface; but to reveal completely the inmost utterance of his heart, this he can never accomplish.

Today, in the cloudy dawn, I hear that inner utterance shaking the chains of the barred door. I wonder: What am I to do? Who is there at whose call my utterance, scaling the barriers of my work, with lamp of melody in hand, shall set out to meet the universe it loves? Who is there at whose glance all my scattered sorrow will be suddenly gathered into a garland of perfect joy and kindled in one flame? Only to her, who looking at me strikes the right melody, can I bring my gifts. At what turn of the road is she waiting for me – that mendicant who will take away all I possess? The sorrow of my inner sanctuary has put on her robes dyed in ochre[1] and wants to take to the open road, the road that leads beyond the confines of my work, trembling with the tread of the unknown beloved of my heart.

NOTE

1 The mendicant, the wanderer of the open road, wears robes of this colour.

3 *The Cloud Messenger*[1]

I

I am near her, yet banished.

This is the tragedy of being too near – for one cannot see the other in her fullness.

On the first day of our union, what did the flute[2] whisper in our ears?

It sang: 'She has come near to me, she who belongs to the far-beyond.'

And it said further: 'Her, whom one cannot hold, even if she is in one's grasp, have I held; her, who is beyond all finding, have I found.'

After that day, why does the flute play no more?

Because I have forgotten the other half of its message. I remembered only that she is near me, but forgot that she also belongs to the far-beyond.

I see only that half of Love which is union; the other half, which is separation, I fail to comprehend.

Therefore that vision of her with which my eyes can never be sated, escapes me – the curtain of nearness hides it.

In the infinite sky that encompasses two human beings, all words are superfluous. That profound silence has to be filled with the music of the flute. The flute cannot play unless it has the vast emptiness of Infinite Space.

That intervening sky between us has become darkened with sorrow, choked with the daily round of petty work and everyday chatter, with worries and sordidness.

Sometimes, when the wind rises on a moonlit night, I wake up and look at the person lying by my side with an aching pain in my heart – I feel that she is lost to me.

How can this separation be bridged – this separation of the infinity which is I, from the infinity which is she?

When I return home at the end of the day's work, who is she with whom I speak? She is just one among the thousand others of everyday life, she is fully known, and there remains no more mystery to fathom.

But hidden within her, where is she, the inexhaustible One, the unique One, my only One? On the edge of what shoreless sea of desire shall I discover her anew?

Can I ever find the rent in the veil of Time through which to speak to her again – the twilight of some idle evening, laden with the heavy perfume of *Mallika* flowers?

II

The first day of the rainy season appeared with its dark shadows of the Eastern horizon. I was reminded of the poet of Ujjayini[3] and longed to send a message to the Beloved.

Let it be carried on the wings of my songs that would conquer the insurmountable barrier of two hearts, too near to each other. But then my songs will have to row back on the stream of time to that first day of our union, athrill to the plaintive melody of the flute, that day which has become one with all the scents and cries of the first Spring and the first rain of Mother Earth, with the deep sighs of the *Ketaki* forest, and the wild self-offering of the *Sal* flowers.

Let the murmurings of the rains, whispering to the leaves of the coconut trees at the edge of the solitary lake, be transformed into the message of my own heart and be carried to the ears of my Beloved, there where she is engrossed in her daily household tasks.

III

Today the infinite sky has stooped down to the green earth begirt with forests. It whispers to her: 'I am thine.'

The earth replies: 'How can that be? You are infinite and I am so small.'

'I have limited myself by the veil of clouds.'

'You have such a wealth of stars. I have no light of my own.'

'Today, I have left behind all my stars and moon and sun; today, only, you are mine.'

'My tear-drenched heart flutters uneasily in the gusts of the storm-driven wind, but you are still, unmoved.'

'Do you not perceive that today my tears are uneasy too? My heart has also turned green, like that green heart of yours.'

Speaking thus, she obliterates the eternal separation of Earth and Sky with the songs of her tears.

IV

With the song of that marriage union of Earth and Sky, let the rains descend upon our separation. That which is unique and indescribable in the Beloved, let it ring out like melodies struck suddenly on a *setar*.[4] Let her cover her forehead with the veil, blue as the colour of the distant horizon. In the look of her dark eyes, let all the tender raintide melodies vibrate in songs.

Let the garland of *Bakul* flowers feel itself blessed twining round and round her plaited hair.

When the dark forest is resonant with the chirp of the crickets, when the little earthen lamp goes out flickering in the gust of the rain-laden wind, let her then leave her all too familiar household round behind and, stealing along the forest path charged with the scent of dead grass, come to the dark night of my solitary heart.

NOTES

[1] The title is taken from that of the famous drama of Kalidasa, which depicts the undying longing of lovers separated by a cruel fate.

[2] On the day of marriage, a small orchestra of wind-pipes plays plaintive melodies all day long in the porch of the bride's home, because the girl-bride leaves the parental home for an unknown destiny.

[3] Kalidasa.

[4] An Indian stringed instrument.

4 *The Voice*

The clouds in the sky break into drops, to be caught in the arms of the dust. Similarly, no one knows whence come girls, to be caught by this earth.

For them the world is so small – and so are men. Within the confines of the little they must let their whole being be caught – all their talk, all their sorrows, all their cares! Hence their heads are veiled, their wrists bangled, and their courtyard is barred. Girls are the *Indrani*[1] of the heaven of limits.

But with what god's amused laughter has this girl, with her unlimited curiosity, been born in our street? Mother calls her 'the little rogue', father 'the madcap'.

Like the runaway waterfall she leaps over the stones of prohibition. Her mind is like the tender leaves of the topmost branches – always tremulous, always restless.

Today I see that unruly child standing motionless, her body leaning against the railings of the veranda – like the rainbow at the end of a rainy day. Her large black eyes are still, like a wet-winged bird on a branch.

I have never seen her so silent. I feel as if a river, suddenly stopping, has become a lake.

A few days ago, the rays of the sun were scorching pale the face of day, the leaves of the tree, a wan yellow, were in a state of dejection.

Then, suddenly, the dishevelled, mad clouds pitched their tents in a corner of the sky. The red rays of the setting sun flashed out like the unsheathed blade of a sword.

At midnight I found the shutters shaking violently, as if the tempest, holding the tassel of the veil hovering over the city, had given it a violent jerk. Rising from my bed, I found the street lights piercing the dense mist of rain, turbid like the eyes of a drunkard. And the strokes of the church bell were heard muffled in the blanket of the pattering rain.

In the morning, the downpour grew still more severe – and the sun remained hidden.

In this rain, the girl from our street stood motionless on the veranda, leaning against the rails.

Her sister came and said: 'Mother is calling.' She only shook her head violently, and her pigtail swayed. Her brother, holding a paper boat, pulled at her hands. She snatched them away. Still her brother pulled her about, trying to make her join in the play. She gave him a resounding slap.

It is raining. The darkness thickens still more. The girl is standing immoveable!

In the very beginning, the first utterings of creation sounded in the language of waters, in the voice of the wind. After billions of years the messages of the past, half-remembered, half-forgotten, called this girl in the limpid voice of raining July. And so she passed beyond all barriers and got lost.

How vast is Time, how vast this world! On this earth so many lives are played out, through countless ages! The far-away, the unbounded, looked into the face of this turbulent girl through the shadow of the clouds, through the melodious sound of the rains.

And she – the very image of eternity with her wide eyes – stood motionless.

NOTE

[1] The goddess enthroned in Heaven, consort of *Indra.*

5 *The Flute*

The voice of the flute is the voice of eternity. It is like the flow of Ganges from Shiva's matted hair onto this earth[1] – the child of heaven playing on the dust of earth.

By the roadside I hear the flute and my mind is moved, in a way that no words can express. That pain I try to compare with joys and sorrows that are known – but they cannot, I find, be reconciled. It is brighter than any smile, than any tears we know.

And I feel that what is known is not real – the Unknown is Reality. Rising early in the morning, I hear the flute playing in the house of the bride.

Where is the harmony between the melody played on this first day of marriage and that of daily life? Hidden discontent; neglect, humiliation and weariness; meanness of petty desires; the strife of ugly callousness; the wound inflicted by baseness that cannot forgive; the dust-covered poverty of common living – in the celestial voice of the flute, there was no trace of all these!

The melody of the song tore away the curtain of these familiar happenings of everyday life. Under the blood-red veil, the bride and bridegroom exchanged their first, shy, blessed look, whose tremor was echoed in the flute.[2]

As the flute played, while the couple exchanged garlands, I cast a glance at the bride – on her neck was a golden necklace; on her feet, anklets; and she stood, as it were, on the lotus of joy, floating on a sea of tears.

Swayed in the melody of the flute, she did not seem to belong to the world of everyday. That girl of the well-known home was transformed into the bride of the Unknown home. The flute says that this is Reality.

NOTES

[1] The Ganges originally flowed in heaven. To purify the earth of its sins, Lord Shiva, whose abode is in the Himalayas, brought down the Ganges from heaven to earth through the strength of his *Tapasya* (meditation). But to break the great shock of this impact, he let the Ganges fall first on his matted hair. Its heavenly origin explains the river's great sanctity to Hindus.

[2] From early dawn on the marriage day, the flute plays in the bride's house where, in the evening, at the hour held auspicious by the astrologer, the marriage ceremony takes place.

6 *Night and Morning*

Here the night descends.

O Lord, the Sun! To what country, to what ocean's shore has your morning gone?

Here, in the dark, the *Rajanigandha*[1] trembles like the newly-wed bride who has unveiled herself before the bridal chamber.

Where blossoms the *Kanak-chapa* flower of early dawn?

Who has awakened, extinguishing the lamp lit in the evening, throwing away the garland woven in the night?

Here, one by one, the doors are locked – there, the windows open.

Here, the boats are moored and the boatman sleeps – there, the boats are spread out in the wind.

They have come out of the inn and, with faces turned eastwards they march.

Their foreheads are touched by the morning light, and their boat for the last crossing is not yet gone.

For them, in window after window, black eyes tender with longing are looking out with steadfast gaze.

The road unfolds before them the red letter[2] of invitation, saying: 'For you everything is ready.'

In their hearts, to the rhythm of their blood, sounds the drum of victory.

Here, everybody in the dusky light has made their last crossing.

In the courtyard of the inn they have spread out their beds – some are alone, some have tired companions.

What lies in front of the road, they cannot see; what lies behind, they whisper of to one another.

While talking, the words come to a stop and they grow silent.

Then, looking into the sky, they see the seven saints.[3]

O Sun, the Lord! To your left is night, to your right morning – bring them together.

Let the shadow of the one take upon its lap the light of the other and imprint upon it one gentle kiss.

Let the melody of morn bless the melody of night[4] and pass away.

NOTES

1 A flower that blossoms at night from *Rajani*, night and *gandha*, scent.

2 In India, letters of invitation (to a marriage, etc.) are generally printed on red paper.

3 Constellation of Ursa Major.

4 In classical Indian music, each period of the day has its distinctive melody.

[22]

7 *The Alley*

Here stretches our cobbled alley. As if it had set out on some search, it turns now to the right, now to the left. But wherever the alley turns, there is always a house in front.

Whenever it glances up, it sees just a strip of sky – narrow and twisted, just like itself.

One day it asked the strip of sky: 'Sister, in what blue city are you a lane?'

At noon the alley sees the sun for only an instant and says to itself: 'I simply cannot understand it!'

The gloomy shadow of the monsoon clouds deepens between the two rows of houses. A torrent of rain rushes along the pavement, and the July downpour drums, as a snake-charmer drums to make his snakes dance. The pavement grows slippery, umbrellas get entangled; suddenly, from the gutters of the roof, water pours down upon the umbrellas and startles everyone.

Bewildered, the alley says: 'It was dry and all was well; why this senseless outrage?'

In spring, when the south wind rushes along the alley blowing papers hither and thither, it turns into a perfect inferno.

Utterly perplexed, the alley asks: 'What demented god causes this drunken orgy?'

All refuse that gathers day after day along its sides – fish-scales, ashes from the kitchen, remains of vegetables, dead mice – the alley knows to be *real,* solid matter! Never does it ask by mistake: 'Why all this?'

Yet when the sun of autumn slants across the terrace and the temple bells ring, it thinks for a moment: 'Perhaps there is something big behind my lines of cobbles after all.'

Meanwhile the hours pass, the clock strikes nine. The maid brings home her purchases for cooking. The alley becomes choked with smoke and kitchen smells. Those who have to be at their desks start to bestir themselves. Then the alley reflects once more: 'Within the confines of my cobbles lies ugly reality. And what I took to be something big is nothing but a dream.'

8 *A Look*

As she was stepping into the carriage, she turned back and gave me a last look. In this vast world, where can I keep this tiny thing? Where can I find a corner where hours, minutes and seconds will not trample it with their steps? The twilight into which fade the golden colours of the clouds – will this look also fade into that twilight?

If it is scattered among the thousand things of everyday life – how can it preserve itself among the rubbish of daily chatter and life's piled-up sorrows?

That look, like an instantaneous flash, has come to me, overwhelming all else. I will hold it in songs, imprison it in rhythm, and keep it in Beauty's Paradise.

In this world, the might of emperors and the wealth of the rich exist only to die one day. But in a tear, is there not immortality, to keep it forever alive?

Music said : 'Then give it to me. I deal neither with the might of emperors, nor with the wealth of the rich; but these small things are my eternal treasure – with them I weave my garland for the neck of the Infinite.'

9 *A Day*

That afternoon comes back to my mind. From time to time the downpour grows feeble; then, suddenly, a gust of wind whips it to fury.

The room has darkened and I have no mind for work. I take in my hand the *setar* and play on it a melody of the rains.

From the next room she comes to the doorway and retires again. Then she enters silently and sits down. In her hand she has a piece of needlework – with bowed head she begins to sew. After a while she ceases and, through the window, looks out into the trees shrouded in mist.

The rain has stopped and my playing has ended. She rises and retires to do her hair.[1]

Nothing has happened; just that one afternoon made up of rain and music, darkness and indolence.

History is littered with tales of emperors, accounts of wars and revolutions. But the tiny incident of one afternoon remains hidden like a rare jewel in the casket of Time. Only two people have heard it.

NOTE

1 Hindu ladies generally have their hair down after their morning bath and only put it up at tea-time.

[29]

10 *Ungrateful Sorrow*

She passed away early in the morning. My mind started consoling: 'All is *Maya.*'[1]

I replied in anger: 'Here in front of me is the table, her sewing box, the flowerpots on the terrace, on the bed, the hand-fan with her name engraved on it – all these are real!'

The Mind said: 'Still, think it over.'

I protested: 'Stop! Don't you see this book in front of me, half-finished, with her hair-pin marking the page? If all this is *Maya,* then why must she be a greater *Maya*?'

The Mind remained silent. My friend came and said:

'That which is good is true, it never disappears. The world holds it fast to its heart, it is a gem.'

Irritated, I answered: 'How do you know that? Is the body not good? That body – where has it vanished?'

Just as a little child strikes his mother in anger, I began beating against everything that was my moral support in this world.

My heart cried out: 'This world is treacherous!'

Suddenly I was startled! Somebody was whispering: 'What ingratitude!'

Through my window I saw the crescent moon rising behind the banyan tree, as if her sweet smile were playing hide-and-seek. From the star-sprinkled darkness came a gentle reproof:

'That I came to you, was that a deceit? Is the shadow that hides me the only truth?'

NOTE

[1] Illusion.

11 *Seventeen Years*

I had known her for seventeen years.

So many comings and goings, so many meetings, so many têtes-à-têtes!

Surrounding those years, so many dreams, so many conjectures, so many hints.

And then, sometimes, when half asleep, the light of the morning star; sometimes the scent of the *Chameli* flower in the dusk of a rainy day; sometimes the tired strains of the *Nahabat*[1] in the last hours of the spring night!

All this had passed round his mind in the course of those seventeen years!

And, mingling with it all, she used to call his name.

The person who responded to this name was not merely the creation of God – he was created out of her seventeen years of knowing him.

Sometimes in love, sometimes in neglect,
sometimes in work, sometimes in leisure,
sometimes in the midst of all, sometimes in privacy –
thus was he built in the heart of one person.

After that, seventeen more years had gone by.

But those days and nights are no longer strung together by the binding thread[2] of that name – they lie scattered. Therefore the days ask me daily:

'Who shall call us together and surround us with her presence?'

I can give no answer – I pause and ponder.

But they, flying away with the wind, say:

'We go searching.'

'Whom?'

They know not whom.

So they wander hither and thither.

Like aimless clouds, they sail across the sea of darkness, and I can no longer see them.

NOTES

[1] A small orchestra, played in a rich man's house.

[2] *Rakhi.* A piece of coloured silk thread tied round the wrist of another person on special occasions, as a mark of friendship.

12 *First Sorrow*

The path that wound along the forest is overgrown with grass today.

In that solitude, from behind me, someone said:

'Can't you recognise me?'

I turned and looked at her.

I said: 'I vaguely remember, but I can't exactly recall your name.'

She said: 'I was yours long ago – that sorrow of yours when you were twenty-five.'

The corners of her eyes were slightly moist, like the reflection of the moon on the lake's waters.

Astonished, I stood still and said:

'That day I saw you dark, like the clouds of July; today you look like the golden image of Autumn. Have you lost all the tears of that day?'

She said nothing – only a slight smile illumined her face.

I understood; everything was said in that smile. The cloud of rainy July had learnt the smile of Autumn's *Shiuli* flower.

I asked: 'Have you still preserved within you the youth I was at twenty-five?'

She replied: 'Look at my necklace.'

I saw: not one petal of that spring garland had withered.

I said: 'Everything else of mine has withered away. But on your neck my youth of twenty-five has not grown pale.'

Slowly she placed the garland on my neck and said:

'Do you remember, that day you said you wanted no consolation, but only sorrow?'

Ashamed, I replied:

'I did. But after that countless years passed away, and I forgot.'

She said: 'That bridegroom, the god who resides in the heart of man – he has not forgotten. Since then, hidden, I have been waiting in the forest glade. Welcome me back.'

I took her hands in mine and said:

'What wondrous, ineffable beauty is this I behold today!'

She said: 'What was sorrow, is transformed today into peace.'

13 *Play of Names*

Quite early he had started to write poetry. With minute care he would rule lines in the margins with ink of gold, and on them paint flowers with ink of red. Inside this frame he would carefully copy his poems; and on the cover, with great flourishes, he would write his name: 'Sri Kedarnath Ghose.'

One by one, he began sending his compositions to the papers. All refused them.

Therefore he resolved that, when money came to him, he would bring out a paper of his own.

After his father's death, all the elders advised him:

'Try to get some work. Don't waste your time writing.'

He smiled faintly, and continued to write. One after another, he published three books.

He had hoped this would create a great stir. But nothing happened.

However, it did create a stir in the mind of one reader.

That was his little nephew. Having just learnt his ABC, he would read aloud from any book that came to his hands.

One day he ran breathless to his uncle with a book. He said:

'Look! Look, uncle! Here is your name.'

The uncle smiled faintly, and gently pinched the child's cheek.

Then he took out of his box another book and said:

'Well, read it.'

The nephew slowly spelt out his uncle's name.

Another book came out of the box, and in it, too, he read his uncle's name.

When he saw his uncle's name in three books, one after another, he was no longer prepared to be so easily satisfied. With outstretched arms he asked: 'Your name is in many, many books – a hundred? forty? seven?'

His uncle winked and said: 'You will see by and by.'

The nephew ran to his old Nanny to show her the three books.

Meanwhile the uncle had also written a play. Sivaji[1] was the hero.

His friend said: 'Surely this play will succeed.'

In his mind's eye he could see all the streets and alleys plastered with the play's title and his name.

Today was Sunday. His theatre-loving friends had gone to see the managers: to ask their opinion.

Eagerly he watched the street for their return.

Sunday was also a holiday for his nephew.

From early morning he had been inventing a new kind of play.

In his distraction, the uncle had taken no notice.

Near the boy's school was a printing press. From there the nephew had secured some leaden type that spelt his own name.

Some letters were small, and some big.

Any book he could get hold of he stamped with his name.

He must astonish his uncle!

He did astonish him. Uncle entered the sitting-room and found the child very busy.

'Well, *Kanai,* what are you doing?' With the greatest eagerness the nephew showed his uncle what he was doing. Not merely three books, but at least twenty-five books were stamped with *Kanai's* name.

What was all this! The lad had no mind for work, only for play.

And what kind of play!

The uncle snatched away from *Kanai* the type he had collected with so much difficulty.

Kanai cried out in anguish, then sobbed, then burst out again violently! He would not be consoled.

His old nurse ran to him and asked: 'Darling, what has happened? *Kanai*! What has happened?'

With choked voice, *Kanai* replied: 'My name!'

Nurse slipped a piece of cake into the child's hands; throwing it away, he cried: 'My name!'

His mother came and said. '*Kanai,* here is your railway train.'

Kanai pushed away the railway train and cried: 'My name!'

One of uncle's friends returned from the theatre.

The uncle rushed to the door and asked 'What news?'

His friends replied: 'They rejected it.'

After a long silence, the uncle said: 'Even if I have to go bankrupt, I shall start my own theatre.'

His friend said: 'There is a football match today. Aren't you coming?'

'No. I am feeling feverish.'

In the afternoon the mother came and said: 'Lunch is getting cold.'

After sunset, his wife came and said: 'Aren't you going to read me your new story?'

'I have a headache.'

The nephew came and said: 'Give me back my name.'

His uncle gave him a resounding slap!

NOTE

[1] The great Maharatta chief who almost shattered the Moghul empire in the eighteenth century.

14 *Story Telling*

As soon as the child could speak, he said: 'Tell me a story.'

Granny began: 'One king's son, one watchman's son, one merchant's son . . .'[1]

The tutor roared: 'Three times four is twelve.'

But just at that moment, the demon in the story gave a louder roar: 'Fee-fo-fum! I like man's flesh' – and the roar of the multiplication table could not reach the child's ear.

The moralist shut the boy in his room and said: 'Three times four equals twelve – this is truth; but one king's son, one watchman's son, one merchant's son – that is not truth, therefore. . . .'

The child has now crossed that lake of the mind whose location cannot be found on any map. The slender raft of 'three times four equals twelve' tries hard to follow the child's flight – but with its rudder of arithmetical tables it cannot catch him.

The moralist thinks that this is nothing but a child's sheer naughtiness – it should be cured with a whipping.

Seeing the tutor acting this way, granny grows silent.

But troubles never end – as soon as one disappears another takes its place. The storyteller came and took his seat. He began with the story of the Princess exiled to the Forest.[2]

When the story reached the point where the she-demon's nose is being chopped off, the moralist said: 'There is no historical proof of this; what *can* be proved is that three times four equals twelve.'

Meanwhile, in the story, *Hanuman*[3] has given a great leap into the sky – a leap so high that History cannot keep up with it.

From primary to secondary school, and from there to college, the purging of the boy's mind went on. But however much the purging continued, his childish longing to be told a story could not be killed.

It is clear from this that, not only in childhood but at every age, Man is a creature who is nourished by 'storytelling'. Therefore all over the world, in every home, in every epoch, in every tongue, there is a gathering of stories which surpasses all else that Man gathers.

The moralist overlooks one fact – the intoxication of storytelling is the intoxication of the Creator. If He cannot be corrected, then there is no hope of correcting Man.

One day, in his workshop, the Creator became busy, making water from fire, earth from water. Creation was drenched in sweat and filled with vapours. The lumps of metal were just taking solid form; all the raw ingredients were lying scattered about, and there was a din of hammers. If, that day, one had taken a look at the Creator, one would never have thought that there was any trace of childishness in Him.

Then – who knows when – life's play began: the grass grew, trees raised their heads, animals ran, birds flew. Some, rooted to the ground, raised their cupped hands in adoration to the sky; some, at liberty, spread themselves across the earth in all directions; some, under the veil of the waters, encompassed the world in a silent dance; others, spreading their wings in the sky – that great carpet spread out for the Sun god – were busy composing their songs of worship.

Thus aeons and aeons passed. Then, on a sudden whim, forty-nine vapours were summoned to the Creator's workshop. Mingling them all, he created Man. After countless ages, his age of storytelling began at last. Long aeons had been spent in Science, in Craftsmanship; now began his age of Literature.

He made Man blossom forth in story after story. The life of animals and birds consists in eating, sleeping and rearing the young; but Man's life is one of storytelling – so much endured, so much experienced, joy and sorrow, the action and reaction of good and evil; such a whirlpool raised by the clash of will against will, of one against ten, of desire against reality, of nature against aspiration. Just as the river is the flow of water, so Man is the flow of a story. So, when man meets man, the first question asked is: 'What is the news? What has happened? What next?' This 'what next' added to 'what next' weaves the story of Man. This makes life's story, Man's history.

History composed by God, and story composed by man – from their mixture man's daily world is created. *Asoka's* story[4] and *Akbar's* story[5] are not the only true ones for Man; the story of the prince who, in search of the treasure of seven kings crosses the seven seas, is no less true; and so is the story of the simple heroism of the devoted *Hanuman*, who did not hesitate to uproot *Ravana's* mountain. For Man, *Durjadhan*[6] is as true as *Aurangzib*.[7] The point is not, which event has the greater truth on its side; that story is truest which, for him, has the greatest ring of truth.

In God's world of literature, Man is man; therefore he is made neither of pure matter nor of pure philosophy – for all his efforts the moralist could not make man forget this truth. At last, in despair, he tried to make a compromise between morality and story, but he never succeeded. In the end the story is spoilt, and morality limps while rubbish accumulates.

NOTES

[1] Lines from a nursery rhyme.

[2] The theme of the *Ramayana,* India's great epic.

[3] The monkey-god, who was devoted to *Rama* and, with his monkeys, helped to rescue *Rama's* wife, *Sita,* from the demon *Ravana.*

[4] and [5] Two great Indian Emperors – one a Buddhist, the other a Moghul.

[6] Mythological king in the *Ramayana.*

[7] Moghul Emperor, grandson of *Akbar.*

15 *The Court Jester*

The king of *Kanchi* set out to conquer *Karnatak.* He was the victor. As war booty his elephants were loaded with sandalwood, ivory, gold and precious stones.

On his way home he sacrificed hundreds of animals in the temple of *Baleyshwari,* whose steps were red with their blood.

After offering his *Pujah*[1] the king is returning – his body robed in crimson, his neck garlanded with *Jaba* flowers, his forehead adorned with sandalwood *Tilak.*[2] He is accompanied only by his Prime Minister and his Court Jester.

At a mango grove along the way, he saw children playing. The king said:

'Let me go and see what they are playing.'

Arranging dolls in two files, the children were playing at war.

The king asked: 'Who is fighting with whom?'

The children replied: 'The *Karnat* against the *Kanchi.*'

The king asked: 'Who is the victor, who the defeated?'

Proudly the children said: 'Victory to the *Karnat,* defeat to the *Kanchi.*'

The face of the Prime Minister turned grave, the king's eyes were red with anger, while the Court Jester guffawed.

The children were still at their play when the king returned with his troops.

The king ordered: 'Tie the children, one by one, against a tree and cane them.'

The parents came running from the village and begged: 'They are innocent, they were only playing, please forgive them.'

The king called his Commander-in-Chief and said:

'I will give this village a lesson, so that they will never forget the king of *Kanchi.*'

Saying this he returned to his fort.

In the evening the Commander-in-Chief appeared before the king. Saluting him, he said:

'O king! The villagers have all been killed, and only the foxes and dogs are left.'

The Prime Minister said: 'The honour of the king has been saved.'

The Court Priest said: 'The Lord of the Universe is our king's ally.'

The Court Jester said: 'O king, please give me leave to go.'

The king asked: 'Why?'

The Court Jester replied: 'I can neither kill nor slay. By the grace of God I can only laugh. If I continue living in His Majesty's court, my laughter will forsake me.'

NOTES

[1] Orthodox Hindu ritual of offering articles of worship to a god or goddess in a temple.

[2] Mark of sovereignty or caste.

16 *The Horse*

When the work of Creation was ending and the holiday bell was about to ring, a new idea came into *Brahma's* head.[1]

He called the storekeeper of his storehouse and said:

'Ho! storekeeper! bring to my workshop a little from each of the five essences.[2] I will create a new living creature.'

With folded hands, the storekeeper replied:

'*Pitamaha,*[3] when from your factory, you created the elephant, the whale, the python, the lion, the tiger, you took no account of your expenditure. All the heavy and hard materials are almost used up. Earth, water and heat are there only in small quantities – only wind and air are still there in as much abundance as you desire.'

The Four-faced[4] pondered awhile and, twisting his heavy curled whiskers, he said:

'Very well, fetch what is still in the storehouse – we shall see.'

This time, while creating the new life, *Brahma* used earth, water and heat very sparingly. He gave it neither horns nor claws; and with the teeth He gave, one could just chew, but not devour. As for the heat that He put into the creature, it was sufficient for some degree of fighting, but it had no real joy in battle. This creature is the horse. It does not lay eggs, though there is talk of that in the market-place;[5] and so it can be called twice-born.[6]

Whatever else *Brahma* did, He stuffed the creature with wind and air. The result is that his mind is turned wholly towards freedom. He wants to run, outstriding the wind, resolved to pass beyond the sky. Other animals run only from necessity – but this one runs without any reason, as if his greatest delight were to run away from himself. He does not want to snatch anything, nor hurt anyone – only to run away. Madly running, he will grow tipsy, intoxicated, exhausted, wear himself to nothing – such is his intention.

The Horse

The learned say that, when among the five essences that constitute the body, wind and air completely predominate over earth, heat and water, this is bound to happen.

Brahma was well pleased. For their habitation He gave some creatures forests; others, caves; but, because He loved to see it run, He gave the horse open plains.

At the edge of the plains lives Man. Whatever Man gains in his scuffles becomes a burden to him. Therefore, when he saw the horse running about the plain, he thought:

'If, somehow, I could tame this beast, it would help me in my marketing.'

One day he lassoed the horse. On his back he put a saddle, in his mouth a bridle. On the horse's back fell the crack of man's whip, its flanks felt the thrust of spurs. And he was groomed as well.

Because, if left free in the open plains he would run away, walls were raised round him. The tiger had his jungle – and the jungle remained his. The lion had his cave – it was not taken away from him. The horse had his plain – but he was prisoned in a stable! The air within him made him yearn for freedom, but it could not save him from captivity.

When he could bear it no more, the horse started kicking against the wall; but the walls were injured less than his hoofs, though the plaster flaked off and began to lose its beauty.

This angered Man. He said:

'What ingratitude! I feed him with grain and water, I engaged an expensive groom to watch him day and night; and yet I cannot win his heart.'

To win his heart, the groom rained such blows on him that his kicking stopped. Man, calling his neighbours, said:

'There is no creature so devoted as this mount of mine.'

Admiring, they said:

'Indeed, he is calm as water, calm as your religion.'

To begin with, he had neither adequate teeth, nor claws, nor horns – now he could no longer kick at the walls or the air. So, to unburden his mind, the horse would raise his head skyward and neigh: 'Chihi-chihi.'[7] This disturbed Man's sleep, and the neighbours thought that it did not exactly show a very devoted frame of mind. All sorts of instruments were invented to stop his mouth. But, unless his breath is stopped, his neighing cannot be completely silenced. So the stifled sound would sometimes break out in a dying gasp.

One day that sound reached *Brahma's* ears. He broke off his meditation and looked down upon the open plain of the earth. No trace of the horse was to be seen.

He called *Jama*[8] and said:

'No doubt this is your doing. You have taken my horse.'

Jama replied:

'Lord of Creation; you always suspect me. Cast your eyes on the quarter where Man lives.'

Brahma saw a narrow space round which walls had risen; within it, the horse was neighing 'Chihi-chihi' in a very feeble voice.

His heart was moved to pity. He said to Man:

'If you do not set free this creature of mine, I shall furnish him with claws like the tiger's – and he will be of no use to you.'

Man replied:

'Fie, fie! That would only encourage cruelty. But whatever you may say, *Pitamaha,* this creature of yours is quite unworthy of freedom. Solely for his own good, at great expense, I built this stable – an excellent stable!'

Brahma insisted:

'You must set him free.'

Man replied:

'Very well! I shall set him free – but only for seven days. If, after that, you do not say that my stable is better for him than your plains, I am ready to rub my nose in the dust.'[9]

Man released the horse but tied his two front legs tightly with ropes. The horse, then, moved with a gait more grotesque than a frog's.

Brahma, dwelling in far off Heaven, could see the horse's movements, but not his hobbled legs. Seeing his own creation walking thus, like a buffoon, made him blush crimson. He said:

'I have indeed made a mistake.'

With folded hands, Man said:

'Now, whatever can I do with this creature? If, O *Brahma*, there is a plain in your paradise, let me rather send him there.'

Perplexed, *Brahma* answered:

'No, no, take him back to your stable.'

Man replied:

'O Lord of Heaven! For Man this is indeed a terrible burden.'

Brahma said:

'In bearing burdens lies the manliness of Man.'

NOTES

[1] The God of Creation, one of the Hindu Trinity.

[2] Earth, water, fire, air and sky, or ether.

[3] Grandfather. Another epithet for Brahma.

[4] Another name for Brahma.

[5] The teller of a tall tale is often told: 'It is nothing but a horse's egg.'

[6] Because it is supposed to be hatched from an egg.

[7] An onomatopoeic word in Bengali.

[8] Ruler of the Dead, Indian Pluto.

[9] An Indian idiomatic expression meaning to humiliate oneself.

17 *A Question*

The father returned from the cremation-ground.

The seven-year-old child – half-naked, a golden amulet round his neck – was standing alone at the upper window of the house in the lonely alley. The father did not know his thoughts.

The morning sun had just kissed the crown of the *Neem* tree; the fruit-seller had passed on his way, hawking his unripe mangoes.

The father came and took the child on his knee.

The child asked: 'Where is mother?'

Turning his head upwards, the father said: 'In heaven.'

That night the father was exhausted with sorrow, and muttered in his restless sleep.

At the doorway, the dim light of the lamp;

on the walls, a couple of lizards.

In front, the open terrace; there the child came and stood.

All around, the houses with their lights extinguished seemed like policemen in some city of demons – asleep as they stood.

The naked child looked at the sky.

His distracted mind was asking someone: 'Where is the path to heaven?'

No answer in the skies. Only, from star to star, the tears of the mute darkness.

18 *The Wrong Heaven*

I

He was a good-for-nothing sort of fellow. He had no work but many hobbies.

Into little wooden casks he would pour mud and inlay it with little shells.

From a distance they would appear like pictures of flights of birds, meadows where cows were grazing, little hills with waterfalls or traces of footpaths.

He suffered no end of humiliation from his relatives. Sometimes, in despair, he would vow: 'No! I must give up my madness.'

But madness would not leave him alone.

II

There are some students who do not work all the year round, and yet they pass their examinations. His was a similar case.

All his life was spent in fancies that could not be called serious work.

Yet, after death, he learned to his dismay that he was to go to heaven.

But ill luck does not leave one even on one's way to heaven. The heavenly envoy, by mistake, had taken him to the heaven of busy people.

In this heaven there is everything but leisure.

Here the men say: 'There is not a moment to breathe freely.'

The women say: 'We are off to work, dear, no time to chat.'

Everybody says: 'Time is so valuable,' but none: 'It is invaluable.'

Everybody sighs: 'One can't stand the strain any longer,' and is happy!

'I am worked unto death,' this complaint is the eternal music of the busy heaven.

This poor fellow finds no escape, nor fits in anywhere.

When he strolls down the way with his mind up in the clouds, the busy people block it.

Whenever he wants to spread his mat and sit down, he is told it is a cornfield, the seeds have already been sown.

He must always move on and be pushed along.

III

One very busy girl comes every morning to fetch water from the heavenly spring.

She rushes down the way like the quick beat of a highly strung *setar*.[1]

She has done her hair in a great hurry, yet a few untamed ones have escaped and peep into the dark sky of her eyes.

The idle good-for-nothing fellow was standing still on one side of the fountain, like an immobile tree.

Just as pity fills the heart of the royal Princess, as she looks down on a beggar from her palace balcony, a like emotion stirred the heart of the girl as she saw him.

She said with compassion: 'Poor thing, you have nothing in hand?'

The idle fellow replied: 'I have no time to work.'

The girl could not understand what he meant and said: 'Do you want to take some work off my hands?'

He replied: 'I have been waiting all the time just for this, to take work from your hands.'

'What work can I give you?'

'Will you give me one of your pitchers in which you carry your water?'

'What will you do with it? Will you draw water?'

'No, I will draw designs upon it.'

The girl replied, irritated: 'I've no time to listen to such nonsense! I am going.'

But how can a busybody cope with an idle fellow? Everyday they meet at the spring, and every time he makes the same request:

'Give me one of your pitchers, I will decorate it.'

At last she had to own defeat, and she had to give him her pitcher.

Round that pitcher the idle fellow began his design – what play of colour, what rhythm of line!

After the decoration was finished, the girl took the pitcher in her hands and turned it round and round, scrutinizing it.

With raised brows she asked: 'What does it mean?'

'It has no meaning.'

The girl returned home with her pitcher.

Hidden from everybody, she looked at it in a hundred different ways, under all shades of light.

At night she would get up from her bed, light the lamp and sit still, gazing for hours at the design.

For the first time in her life she had come across something that had no meaning.

The next day, when she came to the spring, it seemed as if there was some slight languor, some slight hesitation in the busy urge of her steps.

As if the steps, while walking, suddenly lost themselves in thoughts – thoughts that had no meaning.

That day, too, she met the idle fellow waiting at the corner.

She said: 'What do you want?'

He replied: 'Give me some work from your hands.'

'What work can I give you?'

'If you are willing, I would weave a ribbon of many-coloured threads, for you to tie your hair with.'

'What's the use of it?'

'None whatever.'

The many-coloured, richly designed ribbon was finished.

Henceforth, the girl spent hours before the mirror doing her hair. Work was neglected, and time passed by.

IV

After that, by leaps and bounds, big gaps began to appear within the work of the busy heaven. And that gap was filled with songs and tears.

The heavenly Elders became very uneasy. They called a meeting.

They said: 'Never in the history of this place has such a thing ever happened.'

The Heavenly Envoy came and confessed his guilt.

He said: 'I brought the wrong man to the wrong heaven.'

The wrong man was called to the meeting. Looking at his coloured turban and the neat artistry of his flowing dress, they at once realised what a tremendous mistake had been made.

The President announced to him: 'You will have to go back to Earth.'

Taking his palette of colours, and arranging his little bag for departure, he sighed with relief: 'I am going.'

The girl came and said: 'I'll go too.'

The President shook his head in dismay. For the first time he saw something for which he could find no meaning.

NOTE

[1] A stringed musical instrument.

19 *The Attainment of Perfection*

He has taken the vow to attain perfection so that the doors of heaven will open to him.

Therefore, with diligent seeking, he has learnt the '*Mantra*'[1] which shall bring him immortality. Now he meditates on that *Mantra* alone in the forest.

At the edge of the forest dwelt a forest-girl, who lived by gathering firewood. Sometimes she would bring him fruit and, in cups made of leaves, water from the waterfall.

By degrees his *Tapasya*[2] became so severe that he did not touch fruit – birds came and picked at them.

Still more days passed by. Then the water fetched from the waterfall dried away in the leaf-cups – it did not reach his mouth. The forest-girl said: 'What can I do now? All my service is in vain.'

From then on, picking flowers, she would leave them at the feet of the *Tapaswi*,[3] who did not even notice them.

When the midday sun burnt hot, she stood with the end of her *sari* stretched to give him shade. But to the *Tapaswi*, both sun and shade were all one.

When the darkness thickened in the light of the new moon, the forest-girl lay awake watching over him, though there was no danger.

There had been a time when the *Tapaswi*, meeting the forest-girl, would enquire affectionately: 'How goes it with you?', and she would reply:

'Well or ill, what does it matter! But have you no one in the world to look after you? Your mother, your sister?'

He would say: 'I have them all – but what use would their care be? Could they keep me alive forever?'

She would say: 'Just because life is so transient – for that very reason it is worth so much love and care.'

The *Tapaswi* would say: 'I am seeking the way of eternal life; I will make man immortal.'

In this strain he would go on talking without end; it was a monologue – who could comprehend it?

The forest-girl could not understand a word – but like the peacock dancing to the call of the gathering clouds, her heart would grow troubled.

More time passed by. The *Tapaswi* became silent and talked to the girl no more.

More time passed by. The eyes of the *Tapaswi* closed – and looked at the girl no more.

She felt as if millions of miles lay between her and the *Tapaswi*.

Even after thousands and thousands of years, there was no hope whatever of coming a little nearer to him.

So be it! Yet even if there was no hope, her eyes filled with tears. She thought to herself: 'If, during the course of the day, he would just ask once: "How are you?", that would carry me through the day; if he would, only once in the day, accept some fruit and water, my own food would have some taste.'

Meanwhile news reached the heaven of *Indra*[4] that Man aspired to pass beyond the mortal world and reach heaven – such was his arrogance!

In public, *Indra* feigned anger, but secretly he feared. He said:

'The *Daitya*[5] aspired to conquer heaven by strength of arms – therefore war was waged against them. But Man wants to take heaven through suffering – must I own defeat to him?'

Mahendra[6] said to *Menaka*[7]: 'Go, disturb his meditation.'

Menaka replied: 'O Lord of Lords! If by heavenly weapon you defeat mortal man, it means the defeat of heaven. Man's mortal arrow – is it not in the hands of woman?'

Indra said: 'That is true.'

In Spring, as soon as the south wind sways the *Madhavi* creeper, it gladdens. In the same way, when the winds of paradise touched the forest-girl, her whole mind and body thrilled and blossomed into loveliness. Her thoughts circled like bees from their hives, when they scent the honey.

Just then, one stage of the *Tapasya* had ended. Now he would have to retire to a lonely cave. So he opened his eyes.

Before him he saw the forest-girl – a bunch of flowers stuck in her knotted hair, her *sari* dyed golden with *Kusumbha* flowers.

She was like one whom one half recognises, like a melody that is known but whose words are forgotten; like a picture traced only in outline, to which the painter – in a moment of fantasy, who knows when? – adds a stroke of colour.

The *Tapaswi* rose from his mat and said: 'I must go now to a far country.'

The forest-girl asked: 'Why, O Lord?'

The *Tapaswi* said: 'To complete my *Tapasya*.'

With folded hands the forest-girl said: 'Why must you deprive me of the merit I gain by beholding you?'[8]

The *Tapaswi* took his seat again, pondered long, and said nothing.

As soon as her prayer was granted the girl felt as if her bosom were pierced with points sharp as lightning. She thought: 'I am so insignificant, yet why should my words hold him back?' Waking all night, on her bed of leaves, she began to fear herself.

Next day she came and stood with fruits in her hand – the *Tapaswi* stretched out his arm and took them; as soon as she brought water in her leaf-cup, he drank it. Her whole mind filled with joy.

But soon after, as she stood by the *Sirish* tree on the riverbank, tears flowed unceasing down her cheeks. Heaven knows what she was thinking.

Next morning she bowed her forehead to the *Tapaswi's* feet and said:

'Lord, I want your blessing.'

'Why?'

'I shall go far away.'

'May your *Sadhana*[9] find fulfilment!'

One day his *Tapasya* reached fulfilment.

Indra came down and said: 'You have gained the right to heaven.'

The *Tapaswi* said: 'What need have I for heaven any more?'

Indra asked: 'What do you desire?'

The *Tapaswi* replied: 'This forest-girl.'

NOTES

[1] Mystical verses from the Vedas.

[2] Meditation combined with austerities, undertaken to attain a spiritual goal.

[3] One who performs *Tapasya.*

[4] The presiding deity in the Hindu pantheon.

[5] Race of beings who fought the gods.

[6] The great Indra.

[7] A celestial nymph.

[8] *Darshan.* The act of beholding a deity or, as here, a holy man, brings merit to a devotee.

[9] Spiritual self-realization.

20 *Heaven and Earth*

The lamp of earth burns in the lap of Mother Earth.

The evening star looks down upon her wistfully, to watch her light.

That light is like the anxious look of the beloved, lost to itself; it flickers like a fear that throbs within a mother's heart.

That light burns within the heart of the green earth, and trembles with pain in the restless wind.

The voice of the evening star descends from the skies, bringing benediction, and the immortal flame is athirst to burn up in a mortal flame.

21 *Indra's Heaven*

Indra is the supreme God, also called *Devaraj*, and *Mahendra.* The other gods are:

1. Vrihaspati, the divine lawgiver (also called *Suroguro*).
2. Kartikeya, god of war (also called *Devaguru*).

Indra:	*Suroguro*, once we had lost heaven to the *Daityas.*[1] Then, men and gods fought together and saved heaven; but now our danger is far greater – consider this.
Vrihaspati:	*Mahendra*, I do not understand what danger threatens heaven?
Indra:	There is no more heaven!
Vrihaspati:	No more heaven? How can it be? Then where are we?
Indra:	We are living simply on the habits of the past. We are not even aware that heaven has gradually weakened and finally disappeared.
Kartikeya:	How, *Devaraj*? All the pomp and ceremony of heaven continue as before.
Indra:	Yes. The pomp and ceremony increase – but, like the pomp of the sunset, the end is darkness. General of the gods![2] You know well enough, heaven has become such an unreality that even its fear of danger has vanished. I have forgotten the aeons that have passed since the *Daityas* last assailed heaven. For there is nothing to assail. Heaven did exist then, when from time to time it suffered defeat; but from the time. . . .

Kartikeya: Now I begin faintly to understand what you mean.

Vrihaspati: Just as, when one wakes from a dream, one realizes that one was dreaming – so, hearing *Indra's* words, I feel I was wrapped in illusion[3] but am not yet fully awake.

Kartikeya: Shall I say how I feel? In my quiver are the arrows whose weight I carry; all my thoughts are set on my arrows and all seems well. Then someone says: 'Look around you;' I turn and find the arrows there, but there is nothing to aim at. Heaven has lost its aim.

Vrihaspati: We must find the cause of it.

Indra: The soil from which heaven drew the sap to make the flowers blossom – heaven has lost touch with that.

Vrihaspati: What do you mean by 'soil'?

Indra: Once, I remember, man came to heaven and joined in the work of the gods; and the gods, descending to earth, took arms in the war of man. Then, both heaven and earth were real, and that age was called the Age of Reality. If that relation with the earth is severed, can heaven survive in its own immortality?

Kartikeya: And *Devaraj,* the earth too is passing away. Man is being so merged with the earth, that he has no longer any faith in his own heroism – all his trust is only in matter. Over matter he quarrels and fights. Because the pull towards heaven has been relaxed, the immortal soul cannot pierce matter and soar towards the light.

Vrihaspati: What way, then, to save man?

Indra: Heaven and earth must again be united.

Vrihaspati: But all trace of the path by which the gods

went down to earth has long since vanished. I had thought it was better so. For thus it could be proved that heaven is independent and needs no support – it is sufficient unto itself.

Indra: Once everybody believed that; but now we see that it is only through earth's love that heaven can live; without that, it withers away. Through pride in our immortality I had forgotten that truth; therefore all trace of the path by which the gods visited the earth, has vanished away.

Kartikeya: After the defeat of the *Daityas* we prudently made all secure, and heaven is well protected. Since then, all the wealth of heaven has been accumulating there; it is no use to the outside world and it suffers no diminution.

Through aeons and aeons, heaven, with none to oppose it, has grown so prosperous that it has receded far from everything. And so heaven today is alone.

Indra: Whether we have gained or lost, whatever separates heaven from its surroundings brings only frustration. When the great parts from the little, its greatness becomes meaningless and a burden to itself. The light of heaven, separated today from its earthen lamp, becomes a will-o'-the-wisp – a worse punishment than being completely extinguished. Heaven, trying to keep itself unsullied, has imprisoned itself within the high walls of sanctity; like the Ganges[4], bursting those towering walls, it has to flow through the soiled earth to free itself from bondage. Today, my mind is troubled and restless to break through that barrier of separation. I will not let heaven be shut in an enclosure, *Vrihaspati*; it must be merged with the unclean, the fallen, the ignorant, the sorrowing.

Vrihaspati: What then do you want to do?

Indra: I will go to the earth.

Vrihaspati: But the way is closed – that is the trouble!

Indra: As god, I shall not be able to go there; I shall have to be born as man. Just as the meteor, dropping from the sky, first quenches its heavenly light in the heavens and, becoming earth, embraces the earth, so shall I go earthward.

Vrihaspati: Where is there still a family on earth worthy for you to be born into?

Kartikeya: Now the merchant is king; the warrior fights for the merchant; and the Brahmin is the merchant's slave.[5]

Indra: Where I shall be born does not depend upon my wish. Wherever I shall be attracted, there will be my place.

Vrihaspati: But to forget that you are Indra. . . .

Indra: Only by forgetting that shall I, becoming mortal, be able to perform my *Sadhana*[6] as a mortal. . . .

Kartikeya: Till now, I had quite forgotten the existence of this earth; today, hearing your words, my mind is again concerned for it. That slim, green earth, following the trail of sunrise and sunset, how eagerly she gazes at the heaven! What joy I feel in helping to heal the timidity of the timid; what glory in bringing hope to the afflicted. Earth, who wears a crown of jasper and diamond, that beauty robed in a blue *sari* – how could she forget that she is a Queen? She must be reminded again that she is worthy of the *Sadhana* of the gods, that she is heaven's eternally Beloved!

Indra: Going thither, I want to leave this message behind, in the ears of the south wind: that, separated from her, all sweetness has departed from the divine nectar, and the heavenly tree[7] is withered; the ocean that girdles her is heaven's tears and man keeps, eternally, the cry of this separation.

Kartikeya: *Devaraj;* if you permit us, we too would like to go to earth.

Vrihaspati: There, through the veil of Death, let us see for once the splendour of Immortality.

Kartikeya: The ever new play of the divine which *Lakshmi*[8] has spread through her humble earthly home – let us not be deprived of its *Rasa.*[9]

I can see that earth has need of me. Because I am not there, man fights shamelessly for his own ends – not for *Dharma.*[10]

Vrihaspati: And because I am not there, man uses knowledge only for self-interest, not to gain spiritual deliverance.

Indra: That is why I am going there – to open the path for you all. When the time comes, like ripened fruit heavy with your own loveliness, you will be loosened and fall to earth. Wait till then.

Kartikeya: When shall we know, *O Mahendra,* that your *Sadhana* has been fulfilled?

Vrihaspati: Can that happy moment ever remain hidden? When heaven shall resound with the trumpet of Victory – then we shall know. . . .

Indra: Ah *Devaguru*, the trumpet of Victory will

not sound! When tears of tenderness flow from the eyes of heaven, then you will know that my birth on earth has been fruitful.

Kartikeya: Till then, we shall not know, I suppose, where amid the dust you will remain hidden.

Vrihaspati: The savour of the earth lies just in this hide-and-seek. Wealth appears there in the garb of poverty; strength grows there in the lap of weakness; and heroism builds its triumphal arch on the dust of defeat. The possible builds its nest amid the impossible; the earth errs when it esteems only what can be seen; only in the unseen can we put our eternal trust.

Kartikeya: But, O Suroraj! Why is the splendour of your forehead dim today?

Vrihaspati: He who is descending to earth – let the lustre of his glory shine radiantly.

Indra: *Devaguru*, already I feel the travail of a new birth. As a lover goes to meet his beloved, so I go to meet sorrow. Her call has drawn my mind to her. Just as *Sati* was separated from *Shiva,* so has heaven's joy separated itself from earth's sorrow. The anguish of that separation has piled up in my mind.
I depart in order to take that anguish to my heart. Through the nectar of love I shall make that anguish blessed. Bid me good-bye.

Kartikeya: *Mahendra,* open the road for us – we shall all meet there. Today, let heaven take that road of sorrow.

Vrihaspati: *Devaraj,* we are waiting for that call of the road. Break open the path for us to depart from heaven – or else there is no salvation for us.

Kartikeya: Free us, *Devaraj,* free us from the bondage of heaven – build us our way through Death.

Vrihaspati: You are King of Heaven. Today, breaking the meditation of heaven, make known to all that heaven belongs to earth.

Kartikeya: Those who, desiring heaven, have made the *Sadhana* of renouncing the world – you have always tried to make them retrace their steps to earth. Today, heaven itself will have to take that path.

Indra: Through conflict, the path of liberation. . . .

Vrihaspati: The liberation that always, joyfully, welcomes conflict.

SONG

Traveller! O traveller!
Your companions –
They march, they march on.
Absent-minded, I linger in a corner,
Light flashes from time to time.
And, suddenly, I hear footsteps
Under the sky, earth and water.
Traveller! O traveller
While marching along,
Send me a call from the road.
Age after age,
Again and again,
You came to my door.
Therefore, suddenly, do I hear
Your steps,
Within my heart.

NOTES

1 Beings who fought against the gods.

2 Kartikeya.

3 Maya.

4 To purify the earth, through Lord Shiva's *Tapasya* (meditation), the Ganges was brought down to earth from heaven, where it originally flowed.

5 The hierarchy of Caste is as follows: *Brahmin,* the scholar and priest; *Kshatria,* the king and warrior; *Vaishya,* the merchant and tradesman.

6 A difficult word to translate. It is the spiritual goal that one sets oneself; to attain it one undergoes *Tapasya* – meditation and spiritual exercises, combined with austerities.

7 *Paryat.* The flower-tree of paradise, produced at the churning of the oceans by the gods.

8 The goddess who bestows prosperity and wealth, wife of the god *Vishnu.*

9 Flavour. Hence emotional flavour of a work of art.

10 The immutable law of the Universe; Lord Buddha came and set the wheel of *Dharma* in motion. It can also mean the ethical law that holds the world together, i.e., religion.

22 *A Song of Welcome (Agamani)*[1]

Preparations are going on day and night – in the midst of it all there is not a moment of leisure. I pause and ask: 'Preparation for what?'

From time to time I give my Mind a push and ask: 'Is somebody coming?' Mind replies: 'Wait a while. I have to purchase land, collect materials, build houses; don't disturb me now with silly questions.'

I grow silent and start being busy again.

I ponder: There will be an end to acquiring lands, and to collecting materials and to building houses – then, at last, I shall get my answer.

The land grew and grew, materials began to pile up, the seven-storeyed stone house was finished.

I said: 'Now give me an answer to my question.'

Mind replies: 'Oh, for God's sake, wait a moment! I have no time.'

'Why? Still more land, still more buildings, still more equipment?'

'Yes, indeed.'

'Have you not had enough?'

'How can one hold all in this small space?'

'Hold what? Hold whom?'

'We can discuss all that later.'

Still I press the question. 'Is it tremendously big?'

'Indeed it is!'

Even in this large mansion it cannot be contained – nor in this big land!

Again, with feverish energy, I start to work. During the day there is no time for meals, at night none for sleep.

Whoever sees me exclaims: 'An efficient man indeed!'

From time to time a doubt arises in me: 'Perhaps this monkey mind of mine knows no reply to my real problems. Therefore he hides the answer under the load of work. From time to time I wish to stop work; listen attentively whether somebody is coming; build no more, but rather light the lamp at home, amass no more but rather weave a garland while it is still flowering-time.

But I have no confidence in myself. Because my Prime Minister is the *Mind*.

Day and night he weighs and measures things to evaluate their true price. He is constantly saying: 'I can't do without more.'

'Why not?'

'Because it is terribly big.'

'What is terribly big?'

Enough! No more words!

When I press him hard: 'It won't do to evade me thus, you must give me an answer,' he says angrily:

'Why must I give an answer? You only make me neglect my work by asking questions about things whose purpose I do not know and whose meaning is unclear to me. And, please, attend to this – so many lawsuits, so many fights; the whole place overflowing with armed guards and policemen, carpenters and labourers, bricks and mortar everywhere, not an inch of space to rest one's feet. Everything here is clearcut – nothing is left to speculation! Then why ask questions that go beyond all this?'

Listening to this I think: 'The Mind is a clever fellow and I am a fool.'

Again I start carrying bricks in a basket and mixing mortar.

II

Thus the days passed by. My land extended beyond the horizon; my five-storeyed mansions were finished, while the roof of the six-storeyed one was being raised. On such a day the monsoon clouds suddenly disappeared and the dark clouds turned white; from the summit of *Kailash*[2] the wind blew, presaging a holiday mood. The scent of the lotus in *Manoswarovar*[3], like agitated bees, made restless the hours of the day and night. Looking upward, I saw the whole sky smiling down upon the scaffolding of my six-storeyed house.

I became agitated and asked all and sundry whom I met.

'O tell me! From what Palace of Winds is the *Nahabat*[4] playing?'

They replied: 'Leave us alone, we have work to do.'

A mad fellow was leaning against the trunk of a tree with a garland of *Kunda* flowers round his neck. He said:

'The welcome song of Agamani is approaching us.'

What I understood is not clear to me – but I exclaimed:

'Then we have not long to wait?'

He replied, smiling: 'No, it will soon be with us.'

I went to the office and said to my Mind: 'Stop your work now.'

Mind replied: 'How can that be! People will call us idle!'

'Let them do so.'

'What's the matter with you? Have you some news?'

'Yes, I have news.'

'What news?'

'The trouble is, I can't give a clear answer. But news has come. From the shores of *Manoswarovar*, following the trails of light, swarms of wild geese have come.'

Shaking his head, Mind said: 'Where is the tower of the big chariot, the pomp and splendour of a grand procession? I neither see nor hear anything.'

I listened with my ear to the ground to hear better and asked: 'Is he coming?'

From all quarters came the answer: 'Yes, he is coming.'

Anxiously the Mind said: 'What can I do! The roof of my sixth storey is still being raised, and all my furniture has not yet arrived.'

The reply resounded through the heavens: 'Demolish, demolish your six-storeyed house.'

The Mind said: 'Why?'

The reply came: 'Today is the homecoming ceremony of *Parvati* to her father, the Himalaya. Your stone building vaingloriously bars the way.'

The Mind, thunderstruck, remained silent.

I heard further: 'Sweep away all your furniture and all your belongings.'

The Mind said: 'Why?'

'Because your belongings take up all the space.'

'Well, let it be. During my working days I erected a six-storeyed mansion, whereas during my holiday I have to demolish everything. During my working days I went from market to market and collected all the furniture, whereas during my holiday I have got rid of it all. But where is the Tower of the Chariot and all the pomp?'

The Mind looked round in all directions.

What did he see? Autumn's morning star.

Only that?

Yes, just that! And he saw the *Shiuli* flowers in the Shiuli forest.

Only that?

Yes, just that. And he saw the *Doeyl* bird of early dawn swinging its tail.

What else?

A little child laughing and running from her mother's lap into the open light.

'You spoke of the Welcome Song – was it just for him?'

'Yes, for him the flute plays every day, and each dawn, light blooms for him.'

'So much space is needed just for this?'

'Yes, indeed! For your king the seven-storeyed mansion, for your lord the house full of furniture, and for these children the entire sky, the entire world!'

'And the tremendously Big?'

'The tremendously Big dwells just in this little space.'

'This child – what blessing does he bring you?'

'He comes bearing the blessing of God – all the hope of the world, courage and its joy. In his secret quiver is hidden the *Brahmastra*,[5] in his heart is hidden the spear of strength.'

The Mind asked me: 'Well, Poet, could you see something?

Could you understand something?'

I replied: 'For that very purpose I have taken a holiday. All those other days I had no time. Because of that, I could not see, I could not understand.'

NOTES

1 The Song of Welcome that is sung for *Parvati* – daughter of Himalaya and consort of Lord Shiva – when she returns to her father's home. Hence any homecoming song of welcome.

2 The holiest peak of the Himalayas.

3 Name of a lake in Tibet, sacred to pious Hindus. The word also means 'The Holy Lake of the Mind'.

4 A small orchestra of wind-pipes.

5 A fabled weapon, which is infallible.

23 *Life and Mind*

In front of my window the red path winds its way to some distant villages on the horizon. The bullock cart, loaded with goods, squeaks along this road, the *Santal*[1] maidens, carrying bundles of straw on their heads, go to the village market and return in the evening, making the air resonant with their laughter.

But today my mind is not fixed on that highway where the traffic of humanity is carried along.

That part of life which is restless, troubled with worries and busy with human activities, lies dormant today – for my body is ill and my mind is unattached.

The stormy sea is only the sea of the upper layers; deep down, where lies the womb of the earth, the waves cannot carry her message. When the waves die down, then alone does the ocean realize its undivided oneness, of the visible with the invisible, of the upper with the deeper layers!

Similarly, as soon as I took leave of my active life, I found my place in that deeper life where all the cosmic forces have their play. As long as I was hustling along the road, I had no time to throw a glance at the banyan tree, standing silently by the wayside. Taking leave of the road, I have come to my window today, and now our mutual exchange of talk can begin. Gazing silently at me for hours, it seems as if the banyan suddenly becomes restless, as if he wants to say;

'Can you not understand it all?'

I console him by saying:

Yes, I understand it perfectly. Don't be so restless.'

For a time the banyan quietens down. Then, suddenly, he seems to become restless again – the same trembling, rustling and shivering all over.

Again I soothe him:

'Yes, yes! Don't worry – I'm your playmate. In this playground of Mother Earth, through aeons and aeons of time, I too have drunk my fill of the sunlight and shared with you the milk of her breast.'

Then suddenly, I hear the breeze caressing him, and he stammers:

'Yes! Yes! Yes.'

The message that dances in my blood and vibrates in the light of the sky comes to me through the music of the tremulous leaves. That symphony is the music of the whole Universe.

The main note in that symphony is:

'I am, I exist, we all exist.'

It is a joyous message! Every particle of the Universe is thrilling with that joy – the Joy of sheer existence!

Today, with the banyan tree, I have been exchanging just that message of Joy.

The Banyan asks:

'Are you there?'

I reply:

'Yes, I am here my friend.'

II

When my friendship with the banyan began in the spring, its leaves had just sprouted and the rays of the sunlight, like truant boys, could peep through the chinks in the leaves and play hide-and-seek with the shadows of the earth.

Then came the rains of July, pouring down upon the earth. The leaves of the banyan also took on a sombre hue, like the monsoon clouds, and through the thick foliage the sun's rays found no path to enter. In Spring the tree was bare like a penniless girl, today it is full like a woman from a well-to-do home – the very picture of perfect contentment. This morning the banyan asked me:

'Why are you sitting encased in bricks and mortar? Why do you not come out into the open and spread your branches like me?'

I replied:

Man has to harmonize his inner and his outer world.'

The tree shook himself and said:

'I can't follow you.'

'I have two worlds, the inner and the outer.'

'Inner world! Where is this inner world?'

'Within my own barrier.'

'What do you do there?'

'I create.'

'Create inside your barrier! I just don't understand the meaning of your words.'

'Just as a river is formed within the barriers of a bank, similarly creation can only take place within the limitations of the finite. The primordial matter caught within an enclosure becomes a gem here, a banyan tree there.'

'What kind of a thing is this, this barrier that surrounds you?'

'It is my Mind. All that is caught within it, is transformed into creation.'

'Besides our suns and moons, how small must your creation look!'

'One cannot measure it by the suns and moons, for these belong to the outer world.'

'By what scale then will you measure it?'

'By happiness – but, more so, by Sorrow.'

'This breeze blowing from the East speaks to me in whispers, and my whole being answers back in response. But what you said – not a syllable of it could I comprehend.'

'How can I make it clear? As soon as your Eastern wind is enmeshed within the strings of the *Vina*,[2] it becomes another creation. In what vast sky of remembrance this new creation finds its place, I do not know. I feel as if there is another sky, a sky where pain reigns.'

'And its Time?'

'Its time is not the time reckoned by events, but by suffering. Therefore that Time is measureless.'

'You are indeed an unique creature, inhabiting two skies and reckoning two Times! You are beyond my understanding.'

'Need you understand?'

'Do you really understand the language of my world, what you call the outer world?

'When your language is transformed by my inner world, if you want to call it understanding, then it is understanding; if you want to call it song, then it is song; if imagination, then imagination.'

III

The tree, raising all its branches, said to me:

'Stop a moment, the trouble with you is: you think too much and you talk too much.'

Hearing this, I thought to myself: 'It is quite true!'

I said:

'To learn to be quiet, that is why I come to you. But, due to habit, even when I am silent my arguing and debating do not stop, just like one who walks even while asleep.'

I cast away my pen and paper and sat silent, looking at the tree. His tender leaves, like the fingers of an expert musician, struck out melodies from the *Vina* of light flooding the skies.

Suddenly my Mind raised its voice:

'Where is the connecting link between what you are seeing and what I am thinking?'

I chid it sharply:

'Again your questions! Will you stop now.'

I remained silent, gazing at the banyan.

Hour after hour passed away.

The tree said:

'Well, have you at last understood?'

I replied:

'Yes, I have.'

IV

That day passed away in silent contemplation.

Next day my Mind asked me:

'Yesterday, while gazing at the tree, you suddenly exclaimed: 'I have understood'. Can you tell me what you have understood?'

I replied:

'Inside him, the Mind of man has become turbid through worries and anxieties. Therefore, to see Life in its pristine purity, he has to turn to this grass, to yonder tree.'

'And what did you see?'

'I saw what joy Life has in itself. In its leaves, its flowers, and its fruits – what designs has it not drawn, what colours has it not painted, what scents has it not spread!'

Therefore, gazing silently at the banyan tree, I exclaimed:

O King of forests! the first paean of Joy that came out of the heart of Mother Earth at her very birth is echoing in all your branches. The smile of that primeval Age is glistening in your tremulous leaves. In me I feel the stir of that primal Life. I was a prisoner in the net of my own worries, you called out to me:

'Come out into the open life where blows the wind and, like me, bring forth your brush of form, your palette of colours and your cup of nectar.'

My Mind remained quiet for a while, then said a little saddened:

'You always run into ecstasies when you start speaking of Life. The things I garnered with such care, why do you not embellish them?'

'What can I say about them? With their worries and their complications they have pierced the heart of earth with pain and made the sky shriek with their demands. Layer after layer is being added, knot after knot is being tied. Where will it all end? The tree has an answer to it.'

'Indeed! What, may I enquire?'

I said:

'As long as there is no life within, all your garnerings are a mere heap, a burden. As soon as Life touches them, they blend into one and become beautiful. That beauty you see in this tree, and in the strains of the music you hear playing under his shadow.

V

It was the early hour of a far-away dawn.

Life left its bed of sleep. It came out into the arid, lifeless world and set off for the Unknown.

In its body there were as yet no traces of langour, in its mind no worries.

In its armour, there were no traces of dust nor any dents.

That unwearied, calm, unconquerable Life I saw revealed this rainy morning in my banyan tree. Shaking his branches he said:

'Good Morning.'

I replied:

'Prince, how goes your battle against that giant, the desert?'

'Fine! Just look around you.'

I looked, and I saw: to the North the ground tinged green with grass, to the East, ears of corn sprouting, to the South, rows of palms along the bank, and to the West, trees of Mango, Coconut and Mohua, so dense that one could not see the horizon.

I said:

'Prince, you are thrice blessed! You are tender, you are young, while that giant is as hard as he is old; you are tiny, and so are your bows and arrows. Those of the giant are huge, his armour is thick, his club big! And yet, I see, it is your flag that is flying everywhere; you have your foot on the prostrate giant, and even the bare rock has owned defeat.'

'Where did you see all these triumphs?' asked the banyan.

'Your fight I see as peace, your work as rest, your triumph as gentleness. That is why the *Sadhak*[3] comes to meditate under your shade, to find the secret of your effortless victory. In the forest, little schools have sprung up to teach how Life works. Therefore those who are tired rest under your shade, those who are distraught seek your message.'

Hearing my praises, the inner life-spirit of the tree seemed to be pleased and said: 'I have come out to give battle to the giant, the desert. But I have a little brother, where has he disappeared in the din of the battle? A few moments ago, were you not speaking of him?'

'Yes, it is he whom we have named "Mind".'

'He is more restless than I! Nothing satisfies him. Can you give me news of this restless fellow?'

'Yes, I can a little. You battle to survive, he to acquire. And beyond this, another battle is raging – the one for giving up. Your fight is against inert matter, his against penury. There is one last struggle – the war against accumulation. While the battle rages, the result sways in the balance! In this confusion, your green flag gives courage to the warriors.

It sings: 'Victory, victory to Life!'

Higher and higher rises the pitch, from one octave to another. Amid this medley of tunes, your *tambura*[4] plays the basic tune of the primeval Life-Spirit, saying: all melodies will one day merge with a paean of joy into the profound melody of Beauty! All receiving and all giving will blossom like flowers, ripen like fruits.'

NOTES

1 One of the dark pre-Aryan, aboriginal tribes of India.

2 Classical stringed instrument, plucked like the harp.

3 One who is seeking God.

4 One-stringed instrument, playing the basic note.

24 *A Present*

The season of the *Pujah*[1] has come. The store-room is full of presents – *saris* from Benares, gold ornaments; lots and lots of them, and vessels full of sweets and curds.

The mother is sending presents.

The eldest son is a civil servant employed in a distant part of the country. The second son is engaged in business and does not live at home; the other sons have quarrelled among themselves and founded different homes, while the relations are scattered far and wide.[2]

All day long the child of the lap is standing at the outer door and sees the procession of maids and servants passing by, carrying presents in brass trays covered with coloured cloths.

The day ends. All the presents have been carried away. The last glow of the sunset, carrying in a golden platter, the last offering of the dying day, set down on its journey to the starry heavens.

The child returns to his mother and says:

'Mother, you gave a present to everyone, only not to me.'

Smilingly the mother replies:

'All have been given their presents. Now see what is left for you.'

So saying, she kisses his forehead.

Almost sobbing, the child replies:

'Shall I not get any present?'

'When you go far away, then you shall have a present too.'

'And when I am near you, shall I get nothing made with your own hands?'

The mother stretches out her arm and, taking him to her lap, says:

'You are made with my own hands.'

NOTES

[1] Important Hindu festival in September-October, similar to the Christmas season.

[2] Until very recently Hindus lived in communal families, i.e. the sons lived in the paternal home even after marriage. The custom has not yet died out.

25 *Festival of the Chariot*[1]

The day of the chariot festival approaches.

The Queen said to the King: 'Come, let us go to see the Festival of the Chariot.'

The King replied: 'Very well!'

From their stables came the horses, from their stables the elephants.

In serried lines march the peacocks, in serried lines the lancers. The slaves, male and female, walk behind.

Only one was left – her work was to gather forest twigs for making brooms.

The headman came and said to her in pity: 'Come, if you want to join the procession.'

She replied with folded hands: 'I cannot go.'

It came to the King's ears that all were going to the procession except that woman of sorrows.[2]

The King said in pity to his Minister: 'Bring her here.'

Her hut was beside the highway. As his elephant passed it, the Minister called: 'O woman of sorrows, come to behold the god.'

With folded hands she replied: 'How far must I walk? How have I strength to reach the threshold of the god?'

The Minister said: 'Have no fear, you are going with the King!'

She replied: 'God forbid! The King's way is not my way!'

The Minister said: 'What will you do? Is it not your good fortune to see the chariot festival?'

'But I shall! The god comes to my hut in his chariot.'

The Minister laughed and said: 'Where is the trace of the chariot at your door?'

She said: 'His chariot leaves no trace.'

The Minister said: 'Tell me, why.'

She said: 'Because He comes in his chariot of flowers.'

The Minister said: 'Where is that chariot?'

The woman of sorrows pointed to two sunflowers that blossomed on either side of her door.

NOTES

[1] On special occasions, the deity is taken out of the temple and carried in a procession.

[2] *Dukshini*: Very difficult to translate in one word. A woman who is destitute, poor, full of sorrows, one to whom life has been hard (from *duksha*, sorrow).

26 *The First Letter*

These were his first days together with his bride; immediately afterwards he had to leave for a distant place.

As he was leaving, by chance, he saw her hidden tears in the mirror. The mind said: 'Let me return and give a few words of comfort.' But there was not even time for that.

That someone should shed tears because he had to go far away – this was something new for him.

As he walked to his destination, the earth, bathed in the setting sunlight, seemed changed with the anguish of love.

That, in the storehouse of infinite yearning, there should be a portion even for a man like him – this thought filled his heart with wonder!

The place where he had come to work was a hill-station.

Wandering among the shadows of the pine trees, the curving path embraced the hill in silent supplication, and the tiny rills of the cascade seemed to play hide-and-seek, looking for someone.

Today, the traveller sees reflected in nature the picture he had seen mirrored in the glass – the hidden, longing look of his newly-married bride.

Today his wife's first letter has arrived from the village. She has written:

'When will you come back? Come, come, come soon! I clasp your feet in supplication.'

That, in this world of meetings and partings, so much value should be set on his leaving and his return – who could have guessed it? He saw himself standing under the distressed gaze of those two eyes, and his mind became filled with wonder!

Early in the morning, with the letter, he went for a walk along the curving path under the shadow of the pines. The feel of the letter touched his hands, and he seemed to hear someone whisper:

'Without you, the whole heaven of my universe has become drenched in tears.'

He thought: 'Within me, is there something that is worth such tears?'

The sun arose from behind the Eastern green hills. Through the fringe of the dew-drenched pine boughs, the light shone radiant. Suddenly, at a bend of the road, appeared four girls accompanied by two dogs. Whether or not there was something in his appearance, dress or bearing, the two elder girls gave him a slight look of amusement and passed on their way; the two younger ones tried to surpress their laughter, but could not – tittering, they pushed each other and ran away.

At this outburst of laughter, even the rills of the cascade changed their tune. They clapped their hands. With bowed head the stranger from the plains went on his way and thought: 'Is my appearance worth all this laughter?'

That day he could not walk any more. He returned home and, in his solitary room, unfolded and read the letter: 'Come, come, come soon. I clasp your feet in supplication.'

27 *The Meeting with the Fairy*

The Crown Prince had just completed his twentieth birthday – and marriage proposals began pouring in from everywhere, far and near.

The matchmaker said:

'The daughter of the King of *Bahlek* is a beauty indeed – like a rain of white roses!'

The Prince averted his face and made no reply.

The envoy came and said:

'The daughter of the King of *Gandhar* – like a cluster of grapes on a vine, her loveliness overflows her body.'

Feigning a desire to go hunting, the Prince left for the forest. Days passed, weeks passed, he did not return.

The envoy came and said:

'I have just visited the daughter of the King of Cambodia; the lashes of her eyes are curved like the far horizon of early dawn – cool as dewdrops, sparkling with light.'

The Prince plunged into reading the poems of *Bhartihari*[1]; not for a moment did he lift his eyes from the manuscript.

The King said:

'What is the matter? Call the Prime Minister's son.'

The Minister's son came. The King said:

'You are my son's boon companion. Tell me the truth, why has he no mind to marry?'

The Minister's son said:

'Since he has heard the tale of fairyland, his one desire is to marry a fairy.'

The King's Order was issued: all information must be gathered of the whereabouts of fairyland.

All the great scholars were called; all the manuscripts were searched. Shaking their heads, the scholars said in unison:

'Nowhere on any page is there a mention of fairyland.'

Then all the merchants were called to the King's *durbar*. They said:

'Crossing the oceans, we have visited so many islands – *Eladwip, Marichadwip*, the country of the *labanga* creepers; we have visited the *Malayadwip* to gather sandalwood, the pine forests of the Himalayas to gather musk – nowhere did we get any news of fairyland.'

The King said:

'Call the Minister's son.'

The Minister's son came. The King asked him:

'From whom did the Prince hear of fairyland?'

The Minister's son said:

'It was that madcap, Nabin – flute in hand, he roams about the forest. While hunting, the Prince heard from him the story of the land of fairies.'

The King said: 'Well, call him.'

The madcap, Nabin, appeared before the King and presented some forest flowers. The King asked him:

'From where did you hear of the land of the fairies?'

He said:

'I have entrance to it all the time.'

The King asked: 'Where is it?'

'Where your kingdom ends, under the *Chitra*[2] hills, by the shores of the *Kamyak*[3] *lake*.'

The King asked: 'Can one see fairies, then?'

The madcap replied:

'You can see them, but you cannot know them. They live disguised. Only sometimes, as they disappear, they make themselves known for an instant; you cannot catch them.'

The King asked: 'How do you know them?'

The madcap replied:

'Sometimes by hearing a melody, sometimes by seeing a light.'

Irritated, the King said:

'From beginning to end, this is nothing but madness – drive the fellow away.'

The words of the madcap found an echo in the heart of the Prince. Spring had come. On branch after branch, the *Sal* flowers were jostling against each other; and the forest was thrilled with the scent of *Sirish* flowers. The Prince departed alone to the *Chitragiri*.

Everyone asked: 'Where are you going?'

He gave no answer.

A waterfall rushes from the cave and flows down into the *Kamyak* lake. The village people call it the *Udash*[4] waterfall. In a ruined temple, the Prince made his abode.

A month passed. The tender leaves that sprouted on the brambles took a deeper hue, and the forest path became strewn with flowers. The Prince, in a dream at early dawn, heard the melody of a flute. As soon as he woke, he said: 'Today I shall find her.'

Immediately he mounted his horse, followed the course of the waterfall, and reached the shores of the *Kamyak* lake. There he saw a hill girl sitting on the edge of the lotus lake. Her pitcher was filled with water, but she had not yet left the *ghat*.[5] The dark-skinned girl had stuck a *Sirish* flower in her dark hair – it seemed like the first star shining in the twilight.

The Prince dismounted and addressed her:

'That flower behind your ear – will you give it me?'

She was like the doe that knows no fear. Turning her head, she just glanced at the Prince. At that moment, the shadow of something unknown gathered into a still darker hue on her dark eyes – like the dream caressing sleep, like the passage of July clouds on the horizon.

The girl took the flower from her ear and laid it on the Prince's hand, saying: 'Here, take it.' The Prince asked her:

'Tell me truthfully, what fairy are you?'

For an instant she looked at him full of wonder; but the next moment, like sudden autumn showers, she burst into laughter –

wave after wave of laughter, as if it would never end.

The Prince thought:

'At last the dream seems fulfilled – the melody of this laughter seems to be in tune with the melody of that flute.'

The Prince mounted his horse, stretched out his hands, and said: 'Come.'

She grasped his hands and climbed into the saddle. She took it as the most natural thing in the world. Her pitcher, filled with water, remained at the *ghat.* From the *Sirish* branches the cuckoo cooed: 'Ku-hu, ku-hu.'

The Prince whispered in her ear: 'What is your name?'

She replied: 'My name is *Kajari.*'[6]

Together they rode to that ruined temple, near the *Udash* waterfall.

The Prince said: 'Now throw off your disguise.'

She replied: 'We are girls of the forest – we know no disguise.'

The Prince said: 'I am eager to see you in your fairy shape.'

Fairy shape! Again that burst of laughter – wave after wave of laughter!

The Prince thought: 'This melody of laughter keeps tune with the melody of the waterfall. She is my fairy of the waterfall.'

News reached the King's ears that the Prince had wedded the fairy. From the King's palace came the horses, the elephants, the palanquins.

Kajari asked: 'Why all this?'

The Prince replied: 'You must come to the Royal Palace.'

Her eyes grew dim with tears. She remembered that her pitcher was lying at the water's edge; she remembered that in her courtyard she had spread out the grass-seeds to dry; she remembered that her father and brother had ridden away to hunt – it was time for their return; and she remembered that, for her dowry, her mother was weaving a *sari* under a tree and humming a melody.

She said: 'No, I will not go.'

But the drums started beating; the flute played, and the gong; the noise of the kettledrum drowned her words.

At the palace, when *Kajari* got down from the palanquin, the Queen, striking her forehead, cried: 'What kind of fairy is this?'

The King's daughter said: 'Fie, fie, what a disgrace!'

The Queen's maid said: 'Strange indeed is the fairy's dress!'

The Prince said: 'Hold your tongues! The fairy has come to our home in disguise.'

Day followed day; awake in his bed in the light of the full moon, the Prince saw that the disguise of *Kajari* had not in the least stripped off her body. He saw the dark tresses of the dark girl lying dishevelled, and her body, like a sculpture of black marble, flawlessly carved! The Prince sat in silence and thought: 'Where does the fairy lie hidden, like dawn behind the last darkness of the night?'

The Prince felt ashamed before his own people. Even a little anger came over him one day. As *Kajari* was rising one morning from bed, the Prince grasped her hands tightly. 'Today,' he said, 'I will not let you go – reveal your true shape that I may see it.'

At his words the laugh that she had once laughed in the forest came no more to her lips. In an instant her two eyes filled with tears.

The Prince said: 'Will you always deceive me?'

She answered: 'No, no more!'

The Prince said: 'Well, then, at the coming full moon night of autumn, let everyone see the fairy.'

The full moon stands high in heaven within the palace. The palace music of Nahabat[7] plays softly, in tune with the loveliness of the night.

In bridegroom's dress, garland[8] in hand, the Prince enters the hall. Today the exchange of glances[9] was to come.

Across the bed, a white sheet – on it lay masses of white *Kunda* flowers. And, above them, the flooding moon-light!

And *Kajari*?

She was nowhere to be seen.

The flute of the third watch began to play. The moon had sunk towards the West. Gradually the palace filled with relatives.

Where was the fairy?

The Prince said:

'At parting, she reveals her true self. After that you cannot find her.'

NOTES

[1] A famous Sanskrit poet.

[2] Surprising, wonderful, strange.

[3] A lake that grants all one's desires. *Kamyak* also means enjoyable, desirable, lovely.

[4] Making the mind indifferent to worldly matters, listless.

[5] The paved steps that go down to the water's edge, a landing-stage.

[6] Dark as lamp-black.

[7] A small orchestra, played in a wealthy man's house.

[8] The garland that is exchanged with the marriage vows.

[9] *Subha-drishti.* The first exchange of glances between bride and bridegroom during the marriage ceremony, under the cover of a red veil (from *subha,* auspicious and *drishti,* look).

28 *Salvation*

The lonely girl built an altar in a corner of the garden and started to make an image. Slowly she built up the likeness of the man who was in her heart. She looked at it, she thought, and her tears flowed.

But the image that was once clear in her mind slowly became shrouded in a veil. Like the petals of a lotus at night, the petals of her memory also slowly closed, one by one.

She grew angry with herself and was ashamed.

Her austerities became severe; she lived only on fruits and water, and slept on a bed of grass.

The more the image took shape from the depth of her mind, the less likeness it had to the original. It seemed as if it was not the image of one particular man.

The more she tried, the greater grew the difference.

She decorated the image with ornaments; with her tray of offerings, adorned with a hundred and one lotuses, she worshipped it; in the evening she lit a lamp, filled with perfumed oil, in front of it – the lamp was of gold, the oil was expensive!

As the days passed, the ornaments became more crowded, the altar became covered with articles of worship, and the image was hidden.

A boy came to her and said: 'We will play.'

'Where?'

'There where you have decorated your image.'

The girl drove him away, saying: 'Never shall you play there.'

Another boy came and said: 'We will pluck flowers.'

'Where?'

'Why, from the tree that blossoms near the image.'

The girl drove him away, saying: 'Never shall you touch those flowers.'

Yet another boy came and said: 'Hold your lamp and show us the way.'

'Where is the lamp?'

'Why, that lamp which you light before your image.'

The girl drove him away, saying: 'That lamp none of you shall remove.'

One troop of boys went, another troop came

The girl heard the noise of their play and saw their dances. For a moment she became inattentive and was ashamed.

The day of the fair arrived.

The grandfather of the village came and said:

'Dear girl, will you not come to the fair?'

The girl replied: 'I shall go nowhere.'

Her girl companions came and said:

'Come, let us go to the fair.'

The girl replied: 'I have no time.'

A little boy came and said: 'Come, take me to the fair.'

The girl replied: 'I cannot go; my worship is here.'

One night, in her sleep, she seemed to hear the thunderous noise of the ocean. In company after company, men from far and near were on the move – some in chariots, some on foot, some bearing burdens, others throwing them away.'

When she woke in the morning, the song of travellers drowned the song of the birds. Suddenly she thought:

'I too must go.'

At once she remembered: 'I have my worship – I cannot go.'

She ran to that part of the garden where she decorated her image.

But there she found no trace of it. Where the altar had stood, the road now stretched; men poured after men – ceaselessly.

'Where is he whom I had established here?'

Someone in her mind whispered: 'Among those who are on the march.'

Just then, the little boy came and said: 'Hold my hand and take me.'

'Where?'

The boy said: 'Aren't you coming to the fair?'
The girl said: 'Yes, I will come.'

And so the altar, in front of which she used to sit, became the highway and, among all the travellers, she found him who had become lost within the image.

29 *A Short Story*

It seems to me that Man has burnt his future to ashes in the fire of injustice. There, spring shall never come and bring forth new leaves.

From ages past, Man has been building an altar; it brings him the tidings that his god is on his way, and one day will arrive.

On the day when, frantic like a madman, he destroys his age-old altar, the broken altar says: 'There is nothing to hope for; nobody will come.'

Then, all the preparation of ages turns to mere rubbish. Then, from all sides, I can hear: 'Victory, victory to the beast.'

I hear: 'Today it is the same as it was yesterday. Time is like a blindfolded bullock – always the same groaning as it goes round the same oil-mill. This is called creation. It is nothing but the anguished cry of the blind.'

The mind said: 'Then why trouble any more? Let the song be stopped. One can dispute about "what is"; "what is not" is only a theme for music.'

From childhood, I had gazed on the path where the strains of the welcome-song greeted my heart; the path that turned its ear towards the far-away, hoping to hear the rumbling of an approaching chariot – towards that path I turned my eyes today. I felt as if there was no sign of the longed-for guest, nor of a home.

The *Vina* said: 'If along the far-stretching road I have no one to accompany my songs, then drop me by the way.'

Then I looked to the roadside. Startled, I saw a thorn-bush amid the dust – on it there blossomed a single flower.

I cried out: 'O, there is his footprint.'

Then I saw: 'he far-away is talking in whispers to the earth; there is expectation from sky to sky; in the leaves of the palm trees tremulous under the moonlight, through the openings of the bamboo-grove, there pass glances between the waters of the lake and the moonbeams.

The path said: 'Fear not.'

My *Vina* replied: 'Strike up a tune.'

[*Shyamali*, 67]

30 *Sudden Meeting*

With a shock I met her in the railway compartment.

Before, I had often seen her robed in a red *sari*, flaming like the *Dalim* flower. Today she was wearing a black *sari*, with its end drawn over her head. I felt as if the dark colour surrounded her with an atmosphere of the far-away. My whole mind was startled – I perceived that known face surrounded by the solemnity of the Unknown.

Suddenly, putting aside the newspaper, she gave me a silent greeting.

The barriers of social convention dropped and I started a conversation: 'How are you? How is your family?' and so forth.

She remained still, her eyes looking out of the window – as if those looks wanted to avoid the nearness of everyday life.

Her replies were very short – some questions she answered, some not. With the restlessness of her hands she made it quite clear: why all this talk? Far better to remain silent!

I was sitting opposite her, beside her companions; with a movement of the fingers she beckoned me to come and sit by her.

I felt the audacity of her request.[1] I took my seat next to her.

In a soft voice, drowned by the noise of the moving train, she said:

'Please don't take offence – where is there time to be wasted in small talk? You are going far away – we shall never meet again! Therefore, from your lips I want to hear the answer to a question – a question I have never had answered until today. Will you tell me the truth?'

'Yes.'

With her eyes on the distant sky, she asked: 'Our days together, have they vanished completely? Does nothing remain?'

I paused in silence for a moment. Then I replied: 'The stars

are all there in the depth of the daylight.'
A misgiving seized my mind: Have I just been spinning words?
'Enough!' she said, 'Now go back to your seat.'
At the next station she left the train.
I went on alone.

NOTE

1 In India the sexes do not mix so freely.

[*A Fragment*]

31 *The Cloud Messenger*

I remember some English poet saying that we human beings are like islands separated by the vast ocean of tears. When we look at each other across the vast expanse of water, we feel as if we once belonged to one great continent, but now, through some curse, have become isolated by the foaming waves of the tears of separation. When we let our minds wander from the sea-girt moment of the Present into the distant Past illumined by the genius of the poet[1], we feel that there is no gulf of time between us and the maidens plucking flowers on the banks of the *Rebasrupa*, or the travellers by the wayside who, greeting the first heavy-laden clouds of *Ashar*[2], were pierced by a poignant longing for their wives at home. Between us is the deep unity of common humanity, but the cruel separation of Time. Through the poet's blessing, that Past has been transformed into a paradise of immortal Beauty; from our mundane Present we send our cloud-messengers of the Imagination into the distant Past.

But this yawning gulf of separation is not merely between the Past and the Present, between Man and Man. Her with whom I wish to be united dwells on the far, unapproachable shore of her sea of dreams (*Manasarovar*). There I can reach her only through my imagination, through no other way. Where am I and where art Thou? Between us lies an infinite gulf. Who can bridge it? The deathless personality of the Beloved, lying at the heart of the Infinite, who can ever catch sight of it? Today, I get only a passing glimpse of her through words and gestures, failures and mistakes, light and darkness, mind and body, and the turbid flow of life and death! If only a stray wind wafts from thy shores to mine, I am blessed, for I cannot expect more in this vale of Separation. Of this our *Vaishnava*[3] poet sang: 'Clasped in each other's arms, the two weep the tears of eternal separation.' Each one of us dwells on a solitary mountain summit – beyond us lie the sky and the clouds, and the beautiful earth, the river *Rebasrupa,* the city of *Ujjayini* with all its glory, wealth, and luxury; all of which awaken sweet, poignant memories but remain beyond our grasp; awaken desires but do not fulfil them. So far apart are two human souls!

But I feel as if we dwelt once in some realm of the Mind and later were banished from that paradise. Therefore has sung the *Vaishnava* poet: 'Thou who dwellest within me, who has brought thee out?' How could it happen that she, who dwelt in the world of my mind, has left that abode and stands before me? They who were once united in the heart of the all-embracing Mind, are separated now. Therefore, meeting brings their hearts no rest – they are pierced by the pain of separation and athirst with the longing for union.

Oh, solitary dweller of the mountain peak, who gives you hope that, on a full-moon night of spring, in a paradise of ineffable beauty, you will be eternally united with her whom you embrace in your dreams?

NOTES

[1] *Kalidas,* of the court of Ujjayini (2nd century A.D.?), author of *The Cloud Messenger.* This drama, written in Sanskrit, immortalizes for all time the undying longing of lovers separated by cruel fate. In this fragment Tagore recreates this poignant emotion.

[2] The month that ushers in the monsoon season.

[3] A religious sect who worship God as Love, and see in human love a manifestation of divine love.

[*A Fragment*]

32 *The Soul of Literature*

The son of the village Inspector, the son of the merchant, and the Royal Prince all set out in search of the Royal Princess. In fact 'the Royal Princess' symbolizes a state of mind, which is sought after by the three different kinds of intellect man possesses. The one analyzes her scientifically and comes to know her physiology and psychology. But, in this sphere of abstract knowledge, there is no difference between the Royal Princess and countless other women of everyday life. The eyes with which the scientist or the philosopher sees her, watch with no urge of necessity or of emotional enjoyment – there is only scientific curiosity!

On the other hand, the Royal Princess is a woman of many activities – she cooks, she spins and she weaves. In this way of looking at her, the eye with which the merchant's son regards her, there is neither any emotional quality nor any intellectual enquiry – it is only her economic worth that is considered.

The Royal Prince is not a student of Science – he has not graduated in Economics. He has undertaken this perilous journey not in search of knowledge, not in want of wealth, but solely for the sake of the Royal Princess herself! The place of the Royal Princess is not in the laboratory, nor in the market-place, but in that perennial Spring in the heart of Man from which blossom the flowers of Poetry. She who cannot be known nor classified, she who has no worth in the world of cold, everyday reality but can only be felt deeply – her revelation is in Literature, in the Fine Arts. In this realm of art no connoisseur asks her: 'Why art thou here? What is thy purpose?'

He says: 'Thou art thyself – that is enough for me.' The Royal Prince, too, whispered these words into the ears of the Royal Princess. To say just these words, *Shajahan* had to create the Taj-Mahal.[1]

NOTE

1 The mausoleum built by the emperor Shajahan in memory of his dearly-loved Queen Mumtaj.

[*Punascha,* 90]

33 *Camellia*

Her name is Kamala,[1]
I have seen it written on her note book.
She was going in a tram with her brother to college.
I was sitting in a seat behind her.
One could see a side view of her rounded face,
And the stray hairs on her neck under her gathered hair.
On her lap were books.
I did not leave the tram where I should have.

From now on, I time my leaving.
This time does not exactly agree with my office hours,
But it does with theirs –
I often meet them.
I think to myself: if no other relation binds me to her,
At least she is my fellow-traveller.
Bright intelligence shines in her face.
Over her delicate forehead the hair was pulled tightly back –
Those shining eyes looked fearless.
I muse: Why does no sudden danger threaten her,
So that, saving her, I might feel my life significant –
Some trouble in the street,
Some arrogance of a ruffian!
Such happenings are not rare these days,
But my fate is like the turbid waters of a shallow pool,
Big historical events do not happen within its shores,
The harmless days croak monotonously like a frog –
Neither crocodiles nor swans are to be seen on its waters.

One day the tram was crowded,
Next to Kamala sat an Eurasian.

I was longing, without reason, just to knock his hat off
And remove him by force from the tram.
I found no excuse and my hands were restless.
Then he lit a cigar and began smoking.
I approached him and demanded: 'Throw your cigar away!'
He pretended not to hear it,
And began smoking more vigorously.
I snatched away the cigar and threw it into the street.
Clenching his fist, he looked at me threateningly;
He said nothing more, and jumped off the tram.
Perhaps he knew me –
I am a known football player.
The girl blushed red,
Opening her book, she pretended to read;
Her hands were trembling –
She did not even throw a side-glance at the hero.
The clerks going to their offices, all said: 'Well done, Sir.'
Soon afterwards the girl got down
And took a taxi.

Next day I did not see her
Nor the day after;
On the third day I saw
She was proceeding in a rickshaw to college.
I realized that, like a foolhardy fellow, I had acted wrongly.
That girl was well able to take care of herself –
She had no need of me whatever.
I mused: Fate is like the shallow, turpid pond –
Like the croaking of a frog,
The remembrance of my bravery was only mocking me.
I decided, somehow, to undo the mistake.

I got the news that they were going to Darjeeling[2] for the holidays.
That year I also felt the urgent need for a change of air.
They had a small villa – they named it 'Matiya' –

Camellia

It was a bit off the main road,
Hidden behind a tree,
In front stretched the snowy mountains.
Then I heard they were not coming.
Just as I was thinking of returning, I met one of my admirers, Mohanlal –
The fellow was tall and thin, spectacles on his eyes.
In the mountain air of Darjeeling, his feeble digestion functioned a bit better.
He said: 'My sister Tamika
Gives me no rest till I have brought you to see her.'
The girl is like a shadow –
Just enough body to keep her alive.
She pays more attention to study than to food,
Therefore this strange admiration for the captain of a football team.
Alas! what a trick of fortune!
Two days before I left, Tamika said to me:
'I shall give you something, that will remind you of us –
A flower-pot.'
It was a nuisance – but I remained silent.
Tamika said: 'It is a rare, valuable flower-tree;
Only with much care can it be reared in our native soil.'
I asked: 'What is its name?'
She replied: 'Camellia.'
I was startled –
Like a flash another name came to my mind.
Smilingly I said: 'Camellia,
I suppose it is not so easy to win her heart.'
I don't know what Tamika thought – suddenly she was embarrassed,
But felt happy too.

I went home; with this flower-pot.
I found that, as a neighbour, my fellow-traveller was not a very easy companion. In my railway compartment, I hid the

flower-pot in the bathroom.
Let that pass – this journey home;
Let me skip over the trivialities of the next few months.
During the Pujah[3] holidays, the curtain for the comedy was raised in the Santal-Parganas.[4]
The place is small – I do not want to reveal its name –
Those who seek a change of air for their health
Do not know this place.
The uncle of Kamala was Railway Engineer in this hill-station.
He had built a cottage there –
In the shade of the *Sal* trees, in the quarter where squirrels play.
Here, the blue hills are to be seen in the distance –
Nearby a stream trickles along the sands –
In the *Palash* forest the silk worms were in the chrysalis stage.
The buffaloes were grazing –
On their backs rode naked Santal boys.
No houses were to be seen anywhere.
So I set my tent near the river bank.
I had no companions,
Only my flower in its pot, the Camellia.

Kamala has come with her mother.
Before sunrise, in the dew-wet, cool air
She takes her walk through the *Sal* forest, parasol in hand.
The wild flowers brush her feet –
But she does not notice them.
She crosses on foot the dry bed of the river
And under a tree reads a book.
That she recognised me –
This I knew because she ignored me.

One day I saw they were picnicking at the river bank.
I wanted to go and say: 'Can't you use me in any way?
I can fetch water from the river
And gather firewood in the forest.'

I saw a youth in their party –
Wearing shorts and a silk shirt of English design.
He was sitting near Kamala with legs outstretched
And smoking a Havana.
And Kamala, absentmindedly, was tearing to pieces
The petals of a white china-rose.
Nearby was lying an English monthly.
In a moment I realized, in this silent corner of the Santal Parganas,
I was an unbearable superfluity; there was no place for me here.
I would have left immediately, had it not been for work I had to do.
Also, the Camellia would blossom in a few days,
I would feel free to leave only after I had sent it.
All day long I went shooting.
I returned at sunset time, watered the plant,
And reckoned how many days it would yet take to blossom.

Today the time has arrived.
I called the Santal girl,
Who gathered firewood for me.
Through her hands I wanted to send it,
Covered in *Sal* leaves.
I was then inside the tent reading a detective story.
From outside, I heard a sweet voice call: 'Babu,[5] why have you called me?'
Coming out, I saw the Camellia
Adorning the ears of the Santal girl,[6]
Lightening her dark cheeks;
She asked again: 'Why did you call me?'
I replied: 'Just for this.'
After that I returned to Calcutta.

NOTES

[1] This means lotus flower in Sanskrit and Bengali.

[2] A famous summer resort in the Himalayas.

[3] The important Hindu festival in September-October, similar to the Christmas season. Presents are exchanged, and it is a great time for fun and gaiety for children.

[4] A district in Bengal, where the Santals, a pre-Aryan hill tribe,. live. They have magnificent, ebonite-like bodies, and their dance and bubbling gaiety are something to remember.

[5] Bengali for 'Sir'.

[6] Santal girls always wear flowers in their hair.

[*Punascha*, 28]

34 *A Letter*

I send you my writings – a volume packed with poems.

Jostling together, they show themselves all at once in one cage.

Therefore you will find everything in them but the leisurely gaps between the lines.

The poetry that gently descended on the wings of leisure, remained hidden.

If the stars of night were to be plucked from the sky and tightly strung together into a garland, this might fetch a high price; but connoisseurs would know that something beyond price was missing – something that was full of tender meaning.

Imagine a song rising out of the silent heart of leisure – one single, priceless gem!

Must it be enjoyed inside a jewel-box?

In the court of *Vikremaditya*[1], the poet daily chanted his poems.

The demon of the printing-press had not yet smudged with ink the leisurely sky of Poetry, nor was the mass of verse (pressed under a hydraulic mill) swallowed in one gulp, but enjoyed in slow draughts.

Alas, Poetry, meant to be heard, became a book to be read and was banished to the library!

The treasure of eternity is debased in the publisher's market.

There is no way out of this – it is the age of throwing all things together.

Poetry has to go on her tryst, seeking the reader, riding the bus to *Pataldanger.*[2]

With a sigh the mind reflects:

'If I were born in the time of *Kalidasa* – you *Vikremaditya* and I . . . oh, what's the use of saying it?'

I am born as *Kalidasa* of the printing-press.

You are a modern *Malavika,*[3]

You buy and read poetry sitting in an easy chair:

With eyes closed, you are not lost while listening when you have read it, you do not garland the poet, but pay your debt with one-and-six.[4]

NOTES

1 A king whose court was adorned with nine jewels (i.e. poets), of whom Kalidasa was the most famous.

2 A suburb of Calcutta.

3 A heroine in Kalidasa's drama.

4 1s, 6d.

[*Punascha*, 110]

35 *Letter Writing*

You gave me a gold fountain pen and innumerable materials for writing. The small desk of ebony is laden with embossed writing paper in many sizes, enamelled silver paper-cutter, scissors, knife, sealing wax, red ribbon, paperweight, and pencils red, blue and green.

On parting, you said: 'You must write a letter every other day.'

Early in the morning, after my bath, I begin my letter.

Try as I may, I find nothing to write about.

The only news I can give is: 'You have gone away!'

This news is surely known to you – yet I think you do not realize its full import!

Therefore I feel I ought to tell you this news: You have gone away. Every time I begin a letter, I find that this is no ordinary piece of news! I am not a poet – in my language you will neither hear the tremor of my voice, nor see the longing gaze of mine eyes.

The more I write, the more I tear up.

It has struck ten.

Your nephew Baku must go to school – let me go and feed him.

So I write for the last time: 'You have gone away!'

The rest is nothing but scribbles on my blotting pad.

APPENDIX 1

Tagore the Teacher

TRANSLATOR'S DEDICATION

To the sacred memory of my revered teacher
PROFESSOR ALBERT EINSTEIN
who replied to my congratulations on his
fiftieth birthday in 1929 with the
following words:

Your nobly expressed birthday wishes have given me unusual pleasure. It is good that you have preserved your gentle, sensitive outlook on life in our Europe, which is, as it were, drowning in a multitude of meaningless activities. Even our Science is suffering from this defect. Unity and inwardness of vision must remain our aim.

With friendly greetings,

A. Einstein

(Ihre feinsinnigen Glückünsche haben mich asserordentlich gefreut. Est is schön, dass Sie die zarte Lebens-Einstellung in unserem Europa bewahrt haben, das in der nichtigen Vielheit und Geschäftigkeit sozusagen ertrinkt. An diesem Mangel leidet selbst unsere Wissenschaft. Einheit und Innerlichkeit muss das Ziel bleiben.

Freundlich grüsst Sie Ihr

A. Einstein)

Translation of a letter written by Tagore to the mother of the translator, who was a pupil at his school at Santiniketan. Written in 1912, the year in which the mystical poems of the Gitanjali *(which brought him the Nobel prize) were published, it shows how the deep spiritual concerns expressed in Tagore's poetry are also reflected in his work as a pedagogue. May it remind generations of teachers of the nobility of their calling.*

From the day you handed over Aurobindo to me for his education, a lasting bond of love was established between us. Whatever you may intend to do with Aurobindo, from now on you will have to take this relationship into account.

There are many relationships in life which are purely utilitarian – like the hired taxi, we use them only for as long as we need them. But our ties with a place from which our own humanity gains something of lasting value, naturally become both deep and abiding. When we form a bond of a deep and abiding nature with a person or an institution, it consciously or unconsciously preserves us from all pettiness and urges us on towards deeper awareness and fulfilment. Unfortunately such opportunities present themselves only to the few. Those places where our minds can fully spread their roots and draw in the eternal life-giving sap, are rare indeed. And few people have the capacity to establish a true and lasting relationship anywhere. If it is true that Aurobindo has been able to establish such a relationship with our school at Santiniketan, this should cause you happiness rather than concern. I am not saying this because I think that our school has special spiritual powers. The school in itself cannot give much to anybody, but the person who can extract something through his own *Tapasya*[1] is capable of drawing nourishment from every source. To awaken that power of *Tapasya* is the main purpose of all true education. The great majority of people skim over the surface in a very superficial manner – that is where the danger lies! Man finds fulfilment only where he is able to establish a true and deep relationship with life and with the world. Whatever else Aurobindo may or may not have acquired at Santiniketan, he has, in the depth of his soul, realized life as something real and deeply significant. This realization is something so great and sacred that one's heart cannot help but establish a relationship of deep reverence with the place where the realization has taken place. If it had become clear to you that such a feeling of reverence had not been evoked in Aurobindo, this would be certain proof that he was not capable of receiving something great. For this reason I ask you not to feel anxious or worried about Aurobindo.

If Aurobindo had simply developed as an ordinary college student, passing his university examinations, his mind crushed, repeating mechanically what he had learnt from his masters, would this have satisfied you? Do you not have cause to rejoice that the urge to seek out the truth, even if it sometimes causes him to take the wrong path, has become so strong in him? It is not difficult to correct mistakes, but such a genuine hunger for truth is the rarest thing on this earth.

It is undoubtedly true that external attractions frequently enslave our minds, as is often the case with students of ours who go to England and completely lose their bearings there.

But here in Santiniketan there is no such danger. Anything that might enslave the mind by its external attraction is conspicuously absent here. In fact one might say that quite the reverse is true of this place – it is capable of repelling the mind by its very bareness. I was in despair about Aurobindo for a long time. During this time he seemed indifferent to all the influences around him. He was neither applying his mind to his studies nor was I succeeding in awakening his soul towards higher things. But at last, when our *Vidyaly*[2] did touch his heart, it was not as the result of any artificial means or external temptations. No doubt he was gathering food for his mind without our being aware of it, and when that happened the awakening of his soul within his own self began. There is nothing so beautiful or so great in the whole world as this self-awakening – the man who has experienced it can never forget the ecstatic joy it brings!

But truth is something that cannot be tailored to one's own requirements. It has to be left free to follow its own path. If you want to keep a man circumscribed within a particular circle, or limit him by your particular wishes, you have to kill in him the blossoming of this urge towards the realization of truth. When the

Brahmin reigned supreme over the *Sudra*[3] and forced upon him certain activities useful to the former, he not only deprived him of social equality but also barred his passage towards the search after truth.

Surely you are not going to assert that the flowering of man's innermost soul is not greater than all his other needs. This flowering, however inconvenient it may be to society, is the greatest treasure in man's life.

The inner man in Aurobindo has awakened – you will be making a grave mistake if you consider his hunger, his cry, his restlessness, merely as a nuisance. You will never be able to silence or kill it by starvation, punishment or opposition – and if you did succeed, it would be the saddest thing that could ever have happened!

But perhaps I have miscalculated from the start. Perhaps you do not approve the ideal Aurobindo has embraced. He has not turned out as you would have wished, and – no doubt – you are blaming the teaching and influence of this school for it, thinking: 'what is done is done; in future we are going to mark out a new path for him.'

I have no right to raise any objections to this. You have considered what is good for him and will no doubt try to direct his steps towards it. But if you embark on this task out of anger and irritation, you will only be hurting him, without achieving anything. The path of *Mangalam*[4] is not the path of the machine. If you do not try to understand him, he will become more and more incomprehensible to you and draw farther and farther away from you! His state of mind and his age are such that, with mature judgement and great patience – by considering his deepest needs, suffering with his suffering, holding his hands like a dear friend – you will have to lead him. If you hurt him in anger, you will only harm him and begin to lose him.

For my part, I have only this to say: I have perhaps not brought up Aurobindo according to the ideals which you approve, because it was beyond my powers to do so. But please remember this: if the current of his life has turned towards that which is great and noble, this is no mean achievement. He wants to fulfil and realize his life in a noble way, and this is what is of paramount importance – there is no point in being irritated with the particular path he may have chosen to attain his goal.

This *Vidyali*[2] is the place for my life's *Sadhana*[5] – my *Devata*[6] is here, my *Mukti*[7] is here – it is not merely a school.

Today is the last day of the year. Whatever the different paths each one of us may tread, may we keep forgiveness in our hearts. Only this do I claim for myself: I am not trying to shirk responsibility, I am not striding ahead without great effort, and I have not chosen the easy path.

For the rest, He who is the Judge of truth and falsehood, of right and wrong, He alone will judge us all when the time comes.

Yours,

Rabindranath Tagore

Santiniketan
30 Chaitra, 1317 (Bengali era)
April, 1912

NOTES

1 Meditation and inner concentration.

2 The school was called '*Brahma-Vidyalaya*', the place, where one strives to attain to the knowledge of *Brahma* (God).

3 The lowest caste.

4 The Good, the Benign.

5 Spiritual realization.

6 God.

7 Freedom from bondage.

APPENDIX 2

On My Birthday

A selection from *Janmadinay*, poems written by Tagore at various times on the occasion of his birthday (6 May). They were originally published in Bengali in 1941, the year of the poet's death. Numbers in brackets refer to numbers in the Bengali edition.

[5]

Reaching eighty I muse in wonder:
As the stream of light runs down the fire-fall of a billion stars
Flooding the pointless void,
So have I, like some sudden flash in Creation's sacrificial fire,[1]
Risen from the night's unfathomed heart.
To that earth I have come
Where slime – in the ocean's womb
Through long ages – has come to blossom
Into life, showing a multitude of forms.
That shadow of half-light immersed in illusion
Hung, for ages, over the world of beasts –
Creation still incomplete!
At whose ardent waiting,
At the end of many days,
Came man onto the stage of life!
One by one, new lamps are lit,
New meanings find their voice.
Man, in wondrous light,
Beholds his future's unique shape;
On earth's stage,
Act by act, awareness
Grows in gradual unfolding.

I too have dressed myself
To play within that play –
Obeying a call from Fate
To work at tearing this veil away.
This is my greatest wonder!
Bearing what deep secret aim
Rolls the sun around the world –
Mortal home of souls –
Around the sky, the light, the air,
Earth's surface, peaks and sea!
Wound in that mysterious thread

I came into the world
Eighty years ago.
And a few years from now
I shall depart.

21 February, 1941

NOTE

1 The central concern of the early Aryan cult – as the verses of the Rid-Veda show – was sacrifice. Its aim was to propitiate the gods. In the course of the centuries, it was greatly elaborated; later came the mystical identification of god, victim and sacrifice, and it was held that the universe itself arose from primeval sacrifice. (Note after Professor Basham's *The Wonder That Was India.*)

[10]

How little I know of this world!
How many lands, cities, capitals,
How many rivers, mountains, deserts, seas
And many great deeds of men,
And how many creatures and many trees
Remain unknown to me!
In this universe
So much effort, so many provisions.
My mind, within all this,
Holds but a small niche.
Dismayed, I greedily read
Books of travel that are imbued
With vigour that never wears away!
Bright pictures of the world,
Wherever I find them I pick them up,
Trying with alms to fill my mind's poverty.

I am a poet of this earth.
All its sounds, in the tunes of my flute,
Should find their echo –
Yet so many sounds are untouched, missing,
In this practising of tunes.

Through fancy and through imagination,
With the concert of the world's music
I, in hushed moments, often filled
My mind.
Often, through the unheard song they sing,
Remote and snowy peaks,
In that silent, boundless blue
Sent me their invitation.
The unknown star that shines, solitary,
In the Southern sky,
Has touched my sleepless eyes with wondrous light.

The mighty, flodding waterfall of the far-away,
Sent down its melody
To the forest of my mind.
From all sides, into this stream of nature's music
Many poets have poured their song;
With them all, this alone binds me:
I have their company, I share their joy,
Receive the blessing of *Gitabharati*[1]
And the taste of the universe's song.

But Man, innately inward,
Is most difficult to reach,
Having no measure in the outer world;
When heart mingles with heart,
The inner man is known!
I do not always find its door –
Barriers built by my way of life
Bar the way.
The ploughman plows,
The weaver weaves,
The fisherman casts his nets –
Their labour, which is manifold,
Is spread out wide
And sustains the life of the world.
In a little corner
In the eternal exile honour bestows,
I take a high seat in society.
Sometimes I have set foot
On the threshold of their quarter,
But had not the strength to enter;
Life must be joined to life
Or the cargo of songs is in vain.
Therefore I accept the charge
That is brought against me –
The incompleteness of my songs.
I know my songs,

Though they have walked on many paths,
Have not moved everywhere.
That poet who is the peasant's friend,
Who has earned his trust through word and deed,
And who is nearer the earth –
His singing it is I wait to hear.
To the feast of songs
What I cannot give
I take from others' store –
Only let that song ring true
And not with gestures alone
Delude the world.

Come, Poet, of the unknown, the inglorious,
Of the speechless and the dumb,
Give voice to the agony within their hearts!
In this lifeless, songless land –
Where contempt has dried up everything –
Fill, with your life-giving sap
That joyless desert, free the spring
That's buried in their hearts!
Give those a place
Who play but a one-stringed harp,
At the banquet of the Muse.

Those who are dumb in joy, in sorrow,
Those who stand bowed before the world,
Those near and yet remote –
Let me, O gifted One,
Hear within your songs
Their voice.
Remain their kinsman,
In your honour, let them find honour –
I salute you again and again

21 January, 1941

NOTE

1 The goddess of Music.

[13]

Standing on the threshold where Creation's drama unfolds,
I see in sudden flashes
The realm beyond Darkness,
Where immersed I lay
In consciousness of the Great Being –
Unexpressed is He,
Unperceived, Unknown!
In this dawn
The words of the *Rishis*[1] arise in my mind:
'Oh Sun! Remove the veil that covers your light!
In your perfect light
May I see my true self.'
The self that at journey's end,
Mingles its breath with the air,
And transforms the body to dust –
May it not disguised as Truth
Cast a shadow on life's path!

In the playground of this world,
In joy, in suffering,
I have beheld in sudden flashes
The Infinite, behind the veil of the finite.
Have comprehended:
The meaning of this birth lay
In that Beauty ineffable,
In that Song inexpressible!
When the drama ends,
I shall leave behind
in this earth's temple –
My salutation,
My worship,
Whose value death cannot grasp.

25 January, 1941

NOTE

1 The sages of ancient India who composed the Upanishads.

[17]

In days long gone,
When history was not noisy with the day's news,
In the age of silent fame,
Those who, on a morning that pulsed with life,
Set forth on the death-threatening way
To give immortal food of the *Atma*[1]
To remote strangers;
Those who in hundreds failed to reach the goal,
But, tortured with thirst,
Left their bones amid the desert sands,
Or whose traces the sea washed away –
Their lives, on the unattained path, have not been in vain.
They have become one with that great and bodiless Being
Who, unseen, gives strength to the Eternal Man.
Today, in this morning light,
I receive the touch of their compassion,
And I bow to them.[2]

12, December, 1940

NOTES

1 Soul.

2 This poem might refer to the Buddhist monks who, in their thousands, crossed the Pamirs and the arid deserts of Central Asia to bring the message of the Buddha to the Far East.

[18]

Those who
Through manifold sorrow, through the mind's unrest,
Have been shaken and shaken to their Life's foundation,
Who are apathetic –
Let them harken:
Never lose your self;
May you
Find your kin among
Those who have conquered death,
Who light the flame that, above all pettiness,
Burns unquenchable.
Should you belittle them
Then, in the disgrace of that great shame
Shall you remain imprisoned forever.
Honour yourself by honouring them,
Who in this world are worthy of your remembrance.

[28]

My life is nourished by the river,
And through its veins
The gifts of many mountain peaks run down;
Its fields grow richer from many rivers' silt!

The wondrous sap of life
Feeds the fields from many sources.
Its dream and its awakening
Are circled by many streams of songs
That flow from East and West.

The river – messenger of the Universe –
That brings near the Far,
and brings, even to one's door
The welcome of the Unknown,
That river has wound all my birthdays into one!
My nest, moving in its stream,
Freed of fetters,
Floats from shore to shore.
Not twice-born am I,
Nor have I received the sacred thread –[1]
I am but a wanderer.

The tray of my birthday is ever renewed
With gifts from everywhere –
Gifts given away without a thought.[2]

23 February, 1941

NOTES

1 One belonging to a low caste who, unlike the Brahmin boy, has not gone through the ceremony of investitute with the sacred thread. The brahmin is called *dvija* (the twice-born) because his first birth is the physical one from his mother's womb, whereas the second one is the birth into the spiritual world, when he receives the sacred thread.

2 Written in the year of his death, this is the poet's ultimate avowal: he has passed beyond the narrow limits of his own country and the world of Man has become his home.